Life-Study of Colossians

Messages 1-23

Witness Lee

Living Stream Ministry
Anaheim, California

First Edition, October 2000.

ISBN 0-7363-0910-1
(Complete set, softcover)
ISBN 0-87083-152-6
(Messages 1-23, softcover)

Published by

Living Stream Ministry
2431 W. La Palma Ave., Anaheim, CA 92801 U.S.A.
P. O. Box 2121, Anaheim, CA 92814 U.S.A.

Printed in the United States of America

04 05 06 07 08 09 / 8 7 6 5 4 3 2

CONTENTS

LIFE-STUDY OF COLOSSIANS

MESSAGE ONE

THE BACKGROUND AND POSITION OF THE BOOK

In the book of Colossians Christ is unveiled to a fuller extent than in any other book in the Bible. In this short book many terms and expressions are used to describe Christ. Before we consider the revelation of Christ in Colossians, we need to pay attention to the background and position of this book, both of which are crucial.

I. THE BACKGROUND

Three verses, all of which are warnings, enable us to see the situation which caused this Epistle to be written—Colossians 2:8, 16, and 18. Colossians 2:8 says, "Beware that no one carries you off as spoil through his philosophy and empty deceit, according to the tradition of men, according to the elements of the world, and not according to Christ." This verse mentions four negative things which can cause us to be carried off as captives: philosophy, empty deceit, tradition, and the elements of the world. In the eyes of fallen mankind, philosophy is very good; it is the most highly developed product of culture. The elements of the world, elementary principles of certain teachings, may also be highly regarded by society. Nevertheless, philosophy, deceit, tradition, and the elements of the world can cause us to be carried off as prey.

In 2:16 Paul says, "Let no one therefore judge you in eating and in drinking or in respect of a feast or of a new moon or of Sabbaths." Here Paul lists a number of things that are positive: eating, drinking, feasts, new moons, and Sabbaths. He warned the Colossians not to let anyone judge them with respect to these things.

In verse 18 Paul goes on to say, "Let no one purposely defraud you of your prize, in humility and worship of the angels, standing on things which he has seen, vainly puffed up by the mind of his flesh." The prize spoken of in this verse is Christ as our enjoyment. It is possible to be defrauded of this prize through humility, a very positive human virtue.

A. Asceticism Having Saturated the Church at Colosse

The reason Paul gave these warnings was that the church in Colosse had been saturated with asceticism. This asceticism was related to legality of ordinances (2:20-21) and to Judaistic observances (2:16).

B. Mysticism Having Invaded the Church at Colosse

Furthermore, mysticism had invaded the church. This mysticism was related to Gnosticism, which was composed of Egyptian, Babylonian, Jewish, and Greek philosophies (2:8) and to the worship of angels (2:18).

The vital point concerning the background of the book of Colossians is that culture had been brought into the church life. The population of Colosse was a mixture of Gentiles and Jews. The Gentiles and the Jews had different cultures. For the most part, the Gentiles were under the influence of Greek culture with its philosophy. At that time, however, Greek philosophy was no longer pure. Rather it was a mingling of various philosophies. Furthermore, the Gentile culture was at least somewhat blended with Jewish religious concepts.

This mixture of cultures flooded the church at Colosse. The church should be a house filled with Christ and constituted with Him. Instead, the church there had been invaded by culture. To a large extent, Christ as the unique element in the church life was being replaced by various aspects of this mixed culture. The constituent of the church should be Christ and Christ alone, for the church is the Body of Christ.

Therefore, the content of the church should be nothing other than Christ Himself. Nevertheless, the good elements of culture, especially philosophy and religion, had invaded the church and saturated it.

In particular, a type of religious asceticism had made inroads into the church life. Verses 20 and 21, which speak of ordinances regarding handling, tasting, and touching, refer to this. We know that this asceticism was religious in nature because it was related to the worship of angels (2:18). Hence, the asceticism that flooded the church in Colosse was not crude, but refined and cultured.

To some, the worship of angels may seem quite good, far superior to the worship of reptiles, birds, and beasts. Nevertheless, angel worship is idolatry, although a somewhat refined type of idolatry. People of high culture do not worship animals, but they may be open to worship angels. Some justify such a practice by saying that they do not worship idols, but, in humility, worship the heavenly servants of God. Regarding themselves as too low to worship God directly, they may feel that they must worship Him through an intermediary. This concept has been assimilated into Catholicism, which teaches that we may need the help of an intermediary in order to contact God. In principle at least, Catholicism has adopted the practice of using an intermediary in the worship of God.

It is the subtlety of the enemy to flood the church with the elements of culture. This is what he was doing when the book of Colossians was written. His strategy was to send a mixture of Jewish religion and Gentile philosophy into the church and to saturate the church with this cultural mixture. From the human point of view, this culture, particularly its asceticism, was very good. Asceticism has a good purpose and goal; it attempts to enable people to deal with their lusts. However, we must see that Satan's strategy in flooding the church with culture is to use the most highly developed aspects of culture to replace Christ.

Do not think that this phenomenon was limited to the first century. It is still with us today. In today's Christianity Christ has been almost altogether replaced by other things, especially by good things. The name of Christ may be found in Christianity, but the reality of Christ may be absent. Many things have become substitutes for Christ. For example, even the teaching of the Bible is used by the enemy of God as such a substitute for Christ Himself. Many Christians study the Bible without contacting Christ. Due to Satan's subtlety, any kind of Christian work can also replace Christ Himself. Christian work should minister Christ. However, some Christian works make their particular goal a substitute for Christ.

In today's religion some pastors and ministers may allow their own personalities to replace Christ. Certain Christian workers have attractive, powerful personalities. They use their personalities to draw people not to Christ, but to themselves. This is the reason that many Christians compliment and even praise the personalities of certain pastors. Those who do not have such a strong personality may attract people by their niceness or their humility. Christians may choose to attend a particular so-called church because the minister there is kind and sympathetic.

We in the Lord's recovery may substitute the good aspects of our character or behavior for Christ. If anyone who serves the Lord is sinful or proud, others will be frustrated from coming to the Lord. But the natural meekness or humility of such a serving one is even more damaging and frustrating than his sinfulness or pride. Everyone realizes that nothing sinful can be related to Christ. But not many can discern the difference between good character or behavior and Christ Himself. On the contrary, many identify excellent behavior with Christ. Hence, if we are short of revelation, our good character may become a substitute for Christ.

Because the church is composed of human beings, it is difficult for the church to be separated from society, which is a composition of culture. Yes, as the church, we are separated from the world; we are in the world, but not of the world. However, the church must remain in society. The believers should not live like monks or nuns. In order to have the church life, we must have a normal human living. The issue at hand is how a unit of people can be in society without being influenced by culture. How can we be saved from the influence of our cultural background? As believers in the Lord, we do love one another. Nevertheless, we may have a special love for those with a background similar to ours. Through such an influence operating in the church life, Christ is replaced by culture.

When Paul wrote the Epistle to the Colossians, a number of isms were exerting their influence: Judaism, asceticism, mysticism, Gnosticism. These isms were among the highest products of both Jewish and Gentile cultures. Being good things, they spontaneously became replacements for Christ. Therefore, Paul's purpose in the book of Colossians is to show that in the church nothing should be allowed to be a substitute for Christ. The church life must be constituted uniquely of Christ. He should be our only constituent and our very constitution. This is the reason that in this short Epistle a number of elevated expressions are used to describe Christ. For example, He is called the image of the invisible God, the firstborn of all creation, the firstborn from among the dead, and the body of all the shadows. In 3:10 and 11, Paul says that in the new man there is no possibility of having Greek or Jew, circumcision or uncircumcision, barbarian or Scythian, slave or freeman. Rather, in the new man Christ is all and in all. This means that Christ must be everyone and in everyone. In the new man there is no room for Chinese, Japanese, American, British, French, or Germans. Christ must be every one of us. In the new man Christ must be you and me. Not only must culture go, but even we have to go. It is crucial that we see this revelation.

We need to heed Paul's warning to beware of anything that will carry us away from Christ. Sisters, beware of your kindness, gentleness, and sympathy. Beware of any human virtues that replace Christ. Brothers, beware of your sound mind, strong will, boldness, and any other virtues that are substitutes for Christ. What subtlety of the enemy to tempt us into trying to be nice, gentle, mild, or attractive! Nevertheless, many preachers and ministers teach and practice this very thing. It seems that such kind, humble, cultivated people attract others to the Lord. Actually, they succeed only in attracting people to themselves. No one drawn to them is truly gained by the Lord. I am concerned that even in the churches in the Lord's recovery some may be attracted to the church life not by Christ, but by the character or behavior of certain brothers or sisters.

The main point in the Epistle of Colossians is the fact that in the eyes of God nothing counts except Christ. This fact excludes both good things and bad things, both sinful things and cultured things. In particular, it eliminates all the good aspects of culture. We have pointed out again and again that the enemy of God utilizes culture to replace Christ. This is offensive to God. If Satan cannot corrupt us with evil things, God knows that he will try to use the good aspects of culture to replace Christ. Among today's Christians, where can you find a group of believers with whom you can sense nothing but Christ? Among the various Christian groups we see many good points. However, these good things are not the Person of Christ Himself, but something that has replaced Him in a subtle way. For this reason, in many groups of Christians it is difficult to meet Christ. Some may preach Christ or teach the doctrines regarding Christ, but even this preaching and teaching becomes a substitute for Christ Himself. If we have a clear view of the situation among Christians today, we shall realize that the background of the book of Colossians exactly corresponds to today's situation. This book was written for us, not only for the saints at Colosse.

If we have a clear understanding of the background of this Epistle, we shall realize that the only way for us to take is the way of the cross. The cross is both a narrow way and a highway. For those not willing to take the cross, the cross is a narrow way. But for those who are willing to take this way, the cross becomes a highway. In the church we all should be nothing and nobody. This was Paul's attitude when he said that we have died and have been buried. To lay hold of this, we need revelation. Whatever we are, whatever we have, and whatever we do can become a substitute for Christ. The better we are or the more capable we are of doing things, the more Christ may be replaced in our experience. Through the cross, we need to become nothing, to have nothing, and to be able to do nothing. Otherwise, what we are, what we have, or what we can do will become a substitute for Christ. Then in our Christian life Christ will not be all in all. The book of Colossians teaches us that in the church life Christ must be all and in all. Everything that is not Christ must go.

II. THE POSITION

A. The Cluster of Galatians, Ephesians, Philippians, and Colossians Being the Heart of the Bible

Just as there is a heart in our physical body, so there is a heart in the Bible also. The heart of the Bible is not the book of Genesis or the book of Revelation, nor even the Gospels. It is a cluster of four books: Galatians, Ephesians, Philippians, and Colossians. These books were, of course, written according to the inspiration of the Holy Spirit. Furthermore, their sequence in the arrangement of the New Testament books is most significant. If you read the New Testament carefully, you will realize that these four books stand out. Before Galatians is the book of 2 Corinthians. There seems to be no connection between 2 Corinthians and Galatians. However, as we read through the New Testament, we sense that Galatians is the beginning of something new and that this book is connected to Ephesians, Philippians, and Colossians. In particular, Ephesians and Colossians are sister books. When we turn from Colossians to 1 Thessalonians, we also sense that there is no connection between these books. Hence, Galatians, Ephesians, Philippians, and Colossians are a cluster of books that make up the very heart of the Bible.

The essential subject of these four books is Christ and the church. We have seen that the church is composed of human beings who live in society. As such an entity, it is difficult for the church to stay away from the influence of culture. For this reason, in these books concerning Christ and the church, two of them, Galatians and Colossians, show the damage caused by the law, Jewish religion, and other substitutes for Christ such as asceticism, mysticism, and Gnosticism.

B. Galatians Revealing Christ versus Religion with Its Law

According to Galatians, the Jewish religion, the typical religion, was formed according to God's oracle. But this fundamental religion with its law became a replacement for Christ. Hence, in Galatians there is a strong emphasis upon the danger of the law replacing Christ. In Galatians 1 Paul testifies that he was once a leading religionist among the Jews. He was zealous for God and blameless according to the law. But one day it pleased God to reveal His Son, Christ, in Paul. As a result, Paul came to realize that Judaism is contrary to Christ and that Christ is versus religion with its law. Paul could then declare that he was dead to the law and had nothing to do with it. He had been crucified with Christ, and Christ now lived within him (2:20). Furthermore, in chapter six he said that he suffered persecution simply because he did not teach circumcision. Then he went on to say that the world, meaning specifically the religious world, was dead to him and that he was dead to the world. Between Paul and the Jewish religion there was the dividing line of the cross. As far as Paul was concerned, the entire religious world was on the cross. Moreover, to the Jews, Paul also was on the cross. As a man in Christ, he bore upon him the mark of Christ's death. No longer was he in the Jewish religion, but was absolutely in Christ and for Christ. Hence, Galatians reveals that Christ is versus religion, the law, and circumcision.

C. Colossians Unveiling Christ versus Human Philosophies with Tradition and Asceticism

We have pointed out that in Colossians Christ is revealed to the uttermost, much more than in Galatians. In Galatians

Paul speaks of Christ being revealed in us, of Christ living in us, and of Christ being formed in us. But in Colossians he uses a number of special terms for Christ: the portion of the saints, the image of the invisible God, the firstborn of all creation. In this short book, one aspect of Christ after another is unfolded. Therefore, Colossians reveals that Christ is profound and all-inclusive. The all-inclusive Christ transcends our understanding. Our need is to be infused, saturated, and permeated with Him until in our experience Christ is everything to us: our food, our drink, our feasts, our holy days, our Sabbath, our new moon, our everything. We must not allow anything to replace Christ or to be a substitute for Him. This is the central point of Colossians. Whereas Galatians reveals that Christ is versus religion and the law, Colossians reveals that Christ is versus everything because He Himself is the reality of every positive thing.

D. Philippians Stressing the Living Out of Christ

The book of Philippians emphasizes the matter of living Christ. In Philippians 1:21 Paul declares, "To me to live is Christ." For Paul, to live was not human virtues such as meekness or humility; to live was Christ.

E. Ephesians Revealing the Church

Ephesians deals specifically with the church. The issue, the result, of our living Christ is that the church is produced and built up in a practical way.

We all need to spend more time on the four books that compose the heart of the Bible. Viewing these books as a cluster, we see that we should care only for Christ, not for religion or culture. For us to live is not religion, philosophy, or any ism. In our living, Christ must be all and in all. The result of such a living is the church. Therefore, the heart of the Bible, as seen in this cluster of books, is Christ and the church.

LIFE-STUDY OF COLOSSIANS

MESSAGE TWO

INTRODUCTION

Colossians 1:1-8 is the introduction to this Epistle. As the introduction, these verses disclose the purpose and subject of the book. Paul's purpose and subject are not stated explicitly, but rather indirectly through various indications to be found in these verses.

THREE INDICATIONS

The first of these indications is the phrase "the hope which is being laid up for you in the heavens" (v. 5). Another indication is found in the words "the word of the truth of the gospel" (v. 5). Notice that here Paul says the word of the truth of the gospel, not simply the word of the gospel. A third indication is seen in the words "fully knew the grace of God in truth" (v. 6). The word fully is an adverb that modifies the verb knew. What do the words "in truth" modify? According to many versions, this phrase modifies the word grace. Others regard it as an adverb modifying the predicate knew. If we understand truth here as reality, not just as sincerity, then it is correct to regard the words "in truth" as modifying the predicate knew. According to this understanding, Paul is saying that we must know the grace of God in its reality.

THE HOPE BEING LAID UP FOR US

Let us now consider the hope mentioned in verse 5. Hope, faith, and love in verses 4 and 5 are the three things which the apostle stressed in 1 Corinthians 13:13. The emphasis there was on love because of the Corinthian situation. The emphasis here is on hope, which, strictly speaking, is Christ Himself (v. 27), for the revelation of Christ as everything to us.

Some think that the hope that is being laid up for us in the heavens refers to a particular blessing or some kind of glorious enjoyment. When I was young, I was told that, according to John 14, the Lord Jesus is preparing a wonderful mansion for us in heaven and that this is the hope laid up for us. What a mistake! Our hope is Christ Himself. According to verse 27, Christ in us is the hope of glory. On the one hand, He is in the heavens, but, on the other hand, He is in us to be our hope.

FAITH AND LOVE

If we would understand this fully, we need to consider the faith and love spoken of in verse 4. Paul says, "Having heard of your faith in Christ Jesus, and the love which you have unto all the saints." Faith is to realize and receive what is in Christ, love is to experience and enjoy what we have received of Christ, and hope is to expect and wait for the glorification in Christ. Every genuine Christian has faith in the Lord Jesus and love toward all the saints. These two things prove that we are real Christians. Suppose I contact a certain person and tell him that I am one who believes in the Lord Jesus. If he does not respond to me in love, he himself may not be a genuine believer in the Lord. Love for the saints must always go along with faith in the Lord Jesus. They cannot be divorced.

From the time we first believe in Christ, we spontaneously have love for other believers, no matter what their nationality may be. According to my nature and my background, I could never love the Japanese. When I was a youth, I actually hated them because of the damage Japan had caused to China. But after I had been saved and had entered into the Lord's ministry, I was invited to visit some Japanese brothers in Manchuria. I attended a small gathering held in the home of a Japanese believer. As soon as I entered into the room, spontaneously a love for those brothers welled up within me. My hatred for the Japanese vanished. Those brothers believed in the Lord Jesus, and I believed in Him also. Therefore, we could love one another as fellow believers in Christ. This love is not a natural love, but a love that comes out of our faith in the Lord Jesus. We have to love all the saints, just as the Colossians loved all the saints, regardless of their nationality and regardless of whether they were Jew or Gentile.

In the Lord's recovery there are many nationalities. Humanly speaking, it is impossible for us to be one. However, we praise the Lord that no matter what our nationality may be, we love one another because we all have faith in the Lord Jesus. When I contact brothers from Japan, I do not have any consciousness that they are Japanese brothers and that I am a Chinese brother. On the contrary, I simply have the sense that we are all holy brothers in Christ.

LIVING CHRIST AND LAYING UP HOPE

The reason we can love those whom we could never love naturally is that hope is being laid up for us in the heavens. If I had been the writer of Colossians, I would have said "because of the hope in the heavens." Paul, however, inserted the words "being laid up for you." This matter of hope being laid up for us in the heavens is actually very subjective. It has very much to do with our daily living. According to the context, the laying up of hope in the heavens has a great deal to do with how we live today. The more we love the saints, the more hope is laid up for us in the heavens. However, if we do not love the saints, there will be very little hope laid up for us.

Suppose a certain brother loves all the saints, no matter what their nationality or cultural background may be. Another brother, on the contrary, loves the saints selectively, according to his taste and preference. The one loves all who have faith in Christ, whereas the other loves only a select number of the saints. When the Lord Jesus comes, which brother will have the greater hope? Certainly it will be the one who loves all the saints. This indicates that how much hope Christ will be to us depends on our living Christ today.

The more we live Christ now, the more hope will be laid up for us in the heavens for our glorification. However, if day by day we do not live Christ, Christ will be there in the heavens, but He will not be laid up as a glory for us. For example, if you deposit a certain amount of the money you earn in the bank, some savings will be laid up for you in your bank account. But if you fail to earn money and have nothing to deposit in the bank, there will be no savings laid up for you. In the same principle, the amount of hope that is being laid up for us in the heavens depends on how much we are living Christ. We need to be those who love the saints without partiality because of the One who is our hope. Such a living is the laying up for ourselves of hope in the heavens.

In this Epistle Paul seemed to be saying, "Dear Colossians, if you follow the Jewish observances or the Gentile ordinances, you will not lay up anything for yourselves in the heavens as a hope. You need to live by Christ. One day, Christ who is our life will appear in glory. At present, both you and Christ are hidden in God. He is your inner life. But He will appear in glory, and you will appear with Him. However, I must warn you of the importance of living by Christ today."

Yes, in 3:4 Paul says that Christ is our life and that when Christ is manifested, we shall be manifested with Him in glory. But suppose we do not live by Him; instead we live by the self and by our preferences, loving only those saints who match our taste. To love the saints selectively is to live by the self, not by Christ. If we have this kind of living, we shall not be happy when the Lord Jesus Christ appears in glory. Once again I say that how much we shall enjoy Christ as our hope of glory depends on how much we live Him out today. Therefore, the laying up of the hope in the heavens depends on our living.

If we live Christ and are one with Him, we should be able to say, "Lord Jesus, I love You, and I take You as my life and as my person. Lord, I want to be with You in Your glory and see You face to face. I want to enjoy Your presence, even Your physical presence, in a practical way. Lord, I'm waiting for this and I'm expecting this." If you contact the Lord in this way day by day, you will be very happy at His coming.

Suppose, however, that you do not care for the Lord or contact Him. You may not sin or go into the world, but you continually live by the self. You respect the Lord Jesus as the Savior and as the Lord. But although you honor Him, He is not dear or precious to you, and you do not have intimate fellowship with Him. You neither live Him nor take Him as your person. Do you think that, if this is your daily living with respect to the Lord Jesus, you will be excited and shout praises at His coming? Certainly not! Rather, you will withdraw from Him in shame. Whether or not Christ's coming back will be glory to you depends on how much hope you have laid up in the heavens by living Christ today.

CHRIST OUR LIFE

To lay up hope in the heavens is to live Christ and to take Him as our person. Colossians 3:4 is the only verse in the Bible which says that Christ is our life. In John 14:6 the Lord Jesus says, "I am the life." But in 3:4 Paul says that Christ is our life, an expression which is very subjective. Since Christ is our life, we must live by Him and thereby lay up hope for ourselves in the heavens. This is what it means to love all the saints because of the hope which is laid up for us in the heavens.

THE TRUTH OF THE GOSPEL

In 1:5 Paul goes on to say "of which you heard before in the word of the truth of the gospel." The truth of the gospel is the reality, the real facts, not the doctrine of the gospel. The word, not the truth, may be considered the doctrine of the gospel. In our preaching of the gospel there must be not only the word of the gospel, but also the truth of the gospel, which is Christ Himself. Christ, the reality of the gospel, must be the reality in our preaching.

However, in much gospel preaching there is only the word, perhaps the eloquent or persuasive word, but no reality. This means that Christ is not ministered as reality to those who hear. Our gospel preaching must be different. Although we may be slow in speech, the listeners must be able to sense that the reality of Christ is being infused into them. Those under such a preaching of the gospel will soak in Christ as their reality.

We need to tell the Lord in prayer that what we desire is not knowledge in letters, but His presence with Himself being infused into us and ourselves being saturated with Him. We want to be under His heavenly shining. The longer we stay under His shining, the more reality will saturate and pervade us. This is the truth which is Christ Himself.

Because the Colossians had heard the word of the truth, the reality, of the gospel, they could lay up for themselves a hope in the heavens by living Christ in loving the saints. By taking Christ as their life, they could love those whom it was humanly impossible for them to love. They could enjoy Christ as life by soaking Him in as the truth of the gospel. In this way, they could experience Christ as their hope. Therefore, in these verses both the hope and the truth are the Christ we experience subjectively.

THE FRUIT OF THE GOSPEL

Verse 6 continues, "Which is come to you, as also in all the world it is bearing fruit and growing, as also in you, since the day you heard and fully knew the grace of God in truth." The love for the saints is the fruit borne by the gospel. When the gospel is preached in reality, it bears fruit. In those who receive it, it produces love for all believers.

The church in Colosse was composed of both Jews and Gentiles. Humanly speaking, the Jews and the Gentiles despised and hated each other. But after the Colossians had believed in the Lord Jesus, the Jewish believers and the Gentile believers came to love one another. Although such a love is a human impossibility, it is a fruit of the gospel. This gospel which grows and bears fruit is also Christ Himself. It was Christ who was growing in the Colossians from the day they first heard the word of the truth of the gospel.

FULLY KNOWING THE GRACE OF GOD IN TRUTH

In this verse Paul says that the Colossians "fully knew

the grace of God in truth." To know the grace of God fully is to know it in full, not in part. The grace of God is what God is to us and what God gives to us in Christ (John 1:17; 1 Cor. 15:10). Actually, grace is Christ Himself. In the first chapter of the Gospel of John we are told that the Word which was with God and which was God became flesh and tabernacled among us, full of grace and truth (vv. 1, 14). Furthermore, of His fullness we have all received, grace upon grace (v. 16). Truth here means reality. To know the grace of God in truth is to know it in its reality experientially, not just in word or in doctrine mentally. Truth is Christ as reality, and grace is Christ as our enjoyment. As we experience Christ and enjoy Him, Christ as the truth becomes our grace. The way the gospel grows in us and bears fruit is through our enjoying Christ and experiencing Him as our grace.

In these few verses we see that Christ is so much to us: our hope, our truth, our reality, and our grace. Only when Christ becomes grace to us can we enjoy Him and experience Him. The more we enjoy and experience Christ, the more we grow, bear fruit, live by Him, and lay up hope for ourselves in the heavens.

The words "in truth" may be regarded either as an adverb modifying the predicate knew or as an adjective modifying the noun grace. The grace of God is in truth, in reality, not in mere doctrine or knowledge. As we listen to messages given in the Lord's recovery, we often enjoy grace in reality. Through such a ministry of the Word, grace in reality is infused into us. Because this grace is solid and substantial, we can taste it, enjoy it, and live by it.

If we take the words "in truth" as an adverb modifying knew, we see that our knowledge of grace should not be in doctrine, but in reality. This means that our knowing Christ as grace must be in reality. In the gospel Christ is conveyed to us and infused into us both as truth and as grace. We have Christ as our reality, and this reality is our enjoyment. As we live by the Christ whom we experience as truth and grace, we lay up for ourselves hope in the heavens.

A MINISTER OF CHRIST

In verse 7 Paul says, "As you learned from Epaphras, our beloved fellow-slave, who is a minister of Christ faithful for you." Here Paul points out that Epaphras was a minister of Christ. A minister of Christ is not only a servant of Christ who serves Christ, but a serving one who serves others with Christ by ministering Christ to them.

LIFE-STUDY OF COLOSSIANS

MESSAGE THREE

THE APOSTLE'S PRAYER

The subject of the book of Colossians is the all-inclusive Christ. In his introductory word (1:1-8) Paul indicates that Christ is our hope, reality, and grace. In his prayer and thanksgiving (1:9-14) he gives further indications that Christ is the all-inclusive One. Let us first consider Paul's prayer (vv. 9-11) and then his thanksgiving (vv. 12-14).

I. THE APOSTLE'S PRAYER FOR THE SAINTS TO BE FILLED WITH THE FULL KNOWLEDGE OF GOD'S WILL

Verse 9 says, "Therefore we also, since the day we heard of it, do not cease praying and asking on your behalf, that you may be filled with the full knowledge of His will in all spiritual wisdom and understanding." God's will here refers to the will of His eternal purpose, of His economy concerning Christ (Eph. 1:5, 9, 11), not His will in minor things.

A. Concerning the All-inclusive Christ as Our Portion

Years ago, when young saints asked about things such as marriage or employment, I referred them to this verse in Colossians. I told them that they should seek spiritual knowledge in order to know God's will. But the will of God here is not focused on things such as marriage, jobs, or housing; it is concerned with the all-inclusive Christ as our portion. The will of God for us is that we know the all-inclusive Christ, experience Him, and live Him as our life. To know Christ in this way is to have the full knowledge of God's will.

B. In All Spiritual Wisdom

To know and experience the all-inclusive Christ requires all spiritual wisdom and understanding. The words "all" and "spiritual" modify both wisdom and understanding. Spiritual wisdom and understanding are of the Spirit of God in our spirit in contrast to Gnostic philosophy, which is merely in the darkened human mind. Wisdom is in our spirit to perceive God's eternal will; spiritual understanding is in our mind, renewed by the Spirit, to understand and interpret what we perceive in our spirit.

Wisdom is the intuition in our spirit, whereas understanding is the realization in our mind. Through the intuition in our spirit, we sense something concerning Christ. Along with this, we need our mind to interpret what we sense in our spirit in order to have understanding. Then we shall have the utterance to speak forth what we sense and understand. This requires the exercise of all spiritual wisdom and understanding.

The will of God is profound in relation to our knowing, experiencing, and living the all-inclusive Christ. In verse 9 Paul was not praying that the Colossians would know whom to marry, where to live, or what kind of job they should have. His heart was not occupied with such trivial things. In this verse God's will refers to Christ. It was not God's will for the Colossians to follow Judaistic observances, Gentile ordinances, or human philosophies. Furthermore, it was not God's will for them to practice asceticism, to treat the body severely in order to bridle the indulgence of the flesh. God's will for the Colossians was to know Christ, to experience Christ, to enjoy Christ, to live Christ, and to have Christ become their life and their person. God's will for us today is exactly the same. It seems as if Paul was saying, "Colossians, you have been distracted, misled, and defrauded by Gnosticism, mysticism, asceticism, observances, and ordinances. You need to be filled with the full knowledge of God's will. God's will is that the all-inclusive Christ be your portion."

If we know that God's will is for us to be saturated with Christ, then we have the proper knowledge of God's will. Whatever we do should be done in the will of God. We should marry in Christ, work in Christ, and move in Christ. Christ should be our life and our person. This is the will of God.

C. To Walk Worthily of the Lord

In verse 10 Paul says, "To walk worthily of the Lord unto all pleasing, bearing fruit in every good work and growing by the full knowledge of God." Walking worthily of the Lord results from the full knowledge of God's will. If we know that God's will is for us to be saturated with Christ, to take Christ as our life and our person, and to live Christ, spontaneously our walk will be worthy of the Lord. Some think that to walk worthily of the Lord is to be humble, nice, and generous. However, a worthy walk is a walk in which we live Christ. We can be humble, nice and generous without living by Christ. Only by living out Christ can we walk worthily of the Lord. Christ is the will of God, and He should also be our walk.

1. Unto All Pleasing

A walk worthy of the Lord is "unto all pleasing"; it is pleasing to the Lord in all ways. God the Father is pleased with the Son (Matt. 3:17; 17:5). In Galatians 1:15 and 16 Paul says that it pleased God to reveal Christ, the Son, in him. Nothing is more pleasing to God the Father than for us to live Christ. Apart from Christ, nothing can please the Father.

The only time we are fully happy is when we are living Christ. If we are humble or kind in a natural way, we are not happy. But if we take Christ as our life and our person and live Him out, we shall be the happiest people on earth. To live Christ is pleasing not only to the Father, but also to us. The most pleasant thing is to live Christ, to enjoy Christ, and to experience Christ.

2. Bearing Fruit unto Every Good Work

If we walk worthily of the Lord, we shall bear fruit unto every good work. Do not understand this according to the natural concept. Bearing fruit here refers to living Christ, growing Christ, expressing Christ, and producing Christ in every respect. This is the good work Paul has in mind.

3. Growing by the Full Knowledge of God

This kind of work is related to "growing by the full knowledge of God." This knowledge is not the knowledge in letters in the mind, but the living knowledge of God in spirit, by means of which we grow in life. We need such a knowledge in order to live, grow, and produce Christ.

Christ is not only the will of God and our walk, but He is also every good work and even the full knowledge of God. Once again we see that Christ is all-inclusive. The more we get into the book of Colossians, the more we see that Christ is hope, truth, grace, the will of God, and everything to us.

4. Empowered with All Power

In verse 11 Paul goes on to say, "Empowered with all power, according to the might of His glory, unto all endurance and longsuffering with joy." This power is not only the power of Christ's resurrection (Phil. 3:10), but Christ Himself. Within us we have Christ as a dynamo that continually empowers us "according to the might of His glory." This is the might that expresses God's glory; it glorifies God in His might. With this might we are empowered.

By Christ we are empowered "unto all endurance and long-suffering with joy." Because of this marvelous power, we can be joyful even in sufferings. By means of this power we can take with joy whatever may happen to us. We have reason to be joyful because we have the resurrected Christ as the power within us. If we are joyful during times of affliction, we shall not age so quickly. Instead, we shall look younger than our years.

The Apostle Paul did not pray that the Colossians would have the best husbands or wives, the best houses, and the best jobs. Furthermore, he did not pray that the Colossians would be kept from suffering. To the contrary, he prayed that they would be empowered to all endurance and longsuffering with joy; that is, he prayed that they would have the capacity to suffer long with joy. To suffer long in joy is to endure suffering in Christ. Suffering may actually help us to have an increased enjoyment of Christ. Christ is the joy, the endurance, and the longsuffering. Therefore, Paul's prayer is altogether a prayer for the experience of Christ.

II. THE APOSTLE'S THANKSGIVING

A. To the Father

In 1:12-14 we come to Paul's thanksgiving. In his prayer Paul gave thanks to the Father, who is the origin and source of all blessing. By his thanks to the Father, he brings us to his subject—the all-inclusive Christ.

B. For Qualifying Us to Share the Portion of the Saints in the Light

In contrast to many Christians today, Paul did not give thanks for things such as healing, health, housing, family life, or a job. Rather, he gave thanks to the Father for qualifying us "for a share of the portion of the saints in the light." The book of Colossians concerns Christ, the Head of the Body. Hence, the portion of the saints here is the all-inclusive Christ for their enjoyment. The Father has qualified us not to inherit some heavenly mansion, but to have a share in Christ as the all-inclusive portion of the saints. We can boldly declare that Christ is our all-inclusive portion.

The Greek word rendered portion in this verse corresponds to the Hebrew word used for the allotment of the good land. After the children of Israel had entered into the land of Canaan, each of the tribes was given an allotment of the land. Of course, our portion, our allotment, today is not a physical land in Palestine; it is the all-inclusive Christ. How we must thank the Father for giving us Christ as our divine allotment!

Each of the tribes had an allotment of the good land, and the members of each tribe had a share of this allotment. In the same principle, we have a share of the portion of the saints. This means that we all have a share in Christ.

In verse 12 Paul points out that our share of the portion of the saints is in the light. Light here is in contrast to darkness in the following verse. When we were under Satan's authority, we were in darkness. But now we are in the kingdom of Christ, enjoying Him in light.

C. For Delivering Us out of the Authority of Darkness and Transferring Us into the Kingdom of the Son of His Love

Verse 13 is the explanation and definition of how the Father has qualified us for a share of the portion of the saints. This verse says that the Father "delivered us out of the authority of darkness and transferred us into the kingdom of the Son of His love." For Christ to be the Head of the Body, and for us, His believers, to be the members of His Body, He needed to deliver us out of the authority of darkness, the kingdom of Satan (Matt. 12:26), and transfer us into the kingdom of Christ, the kingdom of God's Beloved. This is to qualify us to partake of Christ as our portion.

If we were still under the authority of darkness, we would not be qualified to share in Christ. But the Father has delivered us out of the authority of darkness. Praise Him that we are no longer in the satanic kingdom! Being delivered from the authority of darkness was the first step to be qualified to have a share in Christ.

The second step was to be transferred into the kingdom of the Son of God's love. We have undergone both a deliverance and a transfer. Because Satan is darkness and Christ, the Son of God, is light, therefore Satan's kingdom is the authority of darkness, whereas the kingdom of the Son of God is the kingdom of light. By being delivered out of Satan's kingdom and transferred into Christ's kingdom we have been qualified for a share of the portion of the saints.

D. For the Redemption, the Forgiveness of Sins

In verse 14 Paul continues, "In Whom we have redemption, the forgiveness of sins." The deliverance in verse 13 deals with Satan's authority over us by destroying his evil power, whereas the redemption in this verse deals with our sins by fulfilling God's righteous requirement. The forgiveness of sins is the redemption which we have in Christ. Christ's death has accomplished redemption unto the forgiveness of our sins.

In Christ, the Son of God's love, we have redemption and forgiveness. When we believed in Christ as our Redeemer, God immediately delivered us out of the authority of darkness and transferred us into the kingdom of light. Here in the light we are qualified for a share of the portion of the saints. This means we are qualified to enjoy Christ. Because this qualification is an accomplished fact, there is no need for us to pray about it. On the contrary, with Paul we should simply thank the Father for this. However, there is the need for us to pray concerning knowing the will of God and walking worthily of the Lord unto all pleasing. Now that we are in the kingdom of the Son of God's love, enjoying Him in the light, we must go on to know Him in full and to walk worthily of Him.

The subject of Colossians is the all-inclusive Christ, the Christ who is everything to us. Day by day we may enjoy Him as our portion.

LIFE-STUDY OF COLOSSIANS

MESSAGE FOUR

DELIVERED OUT OF THE AUTHORITY OF DARKNESS AND TRANSFERRED INTO THE KINGDOM OF THE SON OF HIS LOVE

In 1:13 Paul says, "Who delivered us out of the authority of darkness and transferred us into the kingdom of the Son of His love." Paul's word here corresponds to the word given him by the Lord on the way to Damascus. According to Acts 26:18, the Lord charged Paul, "To open their eyes, and to turn them from darkness to light, and from the authority of Satan unto God, that they may receive forgiveness of sins and inheritance among them that are sanctified by faith that is in me" (Gk.). Both in this verse and in Colossians 1:12 and 13 Paul speaks of darkness, light, authority, those who are sanctified, and the portion or the inheritance. No doubt, Paul's word to the Colossians reflects the Lord's word to him at the time of his conversion.

Years ago, I thought that the authority of darkness referred only to evil things such as gambling, stealing, and fornication. Later I realized that the authority of darkness here includes a great deal more than this. In the book of Colossians the authority of darkness refers not to evil things, but to religious observances, Gentile ordinances, and Gnostic philosophy. In chapter two Paul linked idolatry, the worship of angels, to philosophy, mysticism, Gnosticism, and asceticism. Asceticism denotes the practice of treating the body severely in order to bridle the indulgence of the flesh. This kind of practice is found in Hinduism, Buddhism, and Catholicism. As we shall see later, asceticism is of no value against the indulgence of the flesh (2:23). Religious observances, asceticism, and philosophies are not evil. Some observances are even based on God's commandments in the

Old Testament; for example, the regulations concerning eating. Nevertheless, when Paul says that the Father has delivered us out of the authority of darkness, he means the darkness of these very observances, ordinances, philosophies, and ascetic practices. All of us regard gambling casinos as under the authority of darkness. But not many think that philosophies or ethical teachings are also part of this authority. Therefore, it is crucial that we understand Paul's use of this term in the book of Colossians.

I. DELIVERED OUT OF THE AUTHORITY OF DARKNESS

A. The Authority of Darkness Being the Authority of Satan, the Authority of Evil in the Heavenlies

The authority of darkness denotes the authority of Satan. God is light, and Satan is darkness. Satan's authority of darkness is the authority of evil in the heavenlies, in the air (Eph. 6:12). This evil refers to something that is in rebellion against God. The authority of evil, of rebellion, in the heavenlies is the kingdom of Satan, the authority of darkness (Matt. 12:26).

B. Related to Death

Darkness is related to death. Where darkness is, there death is also. This darkness is opposed to light, which is related to life. Satan, darkness, and death stand in opposition to God, light, and life. According to 1 Peter 2:9, we have been called out of darkness into God's marvelous light. Darkness is Satan as death, but light is God Himself as life.

C. Delivered from the Devil, Who Has the Might of Death

To be delivered out of the authority of darkness is to be delivered from the Devil, who has the might of death (Heb. 2:14; John 17:15). We have been delivered from the Devil, Satan, by the death of Christ (Col. 2:15) and by the life of Christ in resurrection (John 5:24).

We have seen that the authority of darkness is the kingdom of Satan and that Satan himself is darkness. The kingdom of Satan is a system. Not everything in this system is evil. On the contrary, many things are good, or at least are considered good by society. Satan uses various things, both good and evil, to systematize people and to keep them in his system. For those who are fond of gambling, Satan uses gambling to systematize them. Therefore, in his kingdom there is a ministry, a department, of gambling. However, Satan realizes that others may appreciate knowledge. In order to systematize them, Satan has a department of knowledge in his kingdom. Most people condemn gambling, but hardly anyone condemns knowledge. If we encourage others to stay away from the evil aspects of Satan's system, we shall be appreciated. Satan systematizes some people by luring them into practicing evil, but he systematizes others through their efforts to suppress evil.

Another department of the kingdom of Satan is the ministry of philosophy. After speaking of the authority of darkness, Paul goes on to mention ordinances, observances, philosophies, and the elements of the world, all of which are aspects of this satanic authority. Today a great many people are held under Satan's control by philosophy. For this reason, it is often easier to bring a gambler to Christ than a person devoted to philosophy. In China we found it difficult to convert the followers of Confucius. Satan used the ethical teachings of Confucianism to systematize and to control large numbers of Chinese. Satan controlled them and kept them under his authority through ethical philosophy.

The Jews and the Moslems vigorously oppose the gospel of Christ. The Moslems are controlled not by evil things, but by the principles of Islam. In a sense, these principles are good; however, in another sense, they are dreadful.

Mormons, who are known to be honest, ethical, and moral in their daily living, also are controlled by seemingly good things. The Mormons not only refrain from drinking alcoholic beverages, but do not even drink coffee or tea. How strict and upright they seem to be! However, Mormonism is part of the authority of darkness, and the Mormons are held and controlled in darkness by Satan.

At the time of Paul, Judaism had become a major part of the authority of darkness. When Paul, a leading religionist in Judaism, was on the road to Damascus, he was fully under this authority. Then the Lord appeared to him and charged him to open the eyes of others so that they might turn from darkness to light. As a result of Paul's confrontation with Christ, he was blinded temporarily. This blindness indicated that he was formerly among the blind. Now, having been brought to Christ, he must seek to turn others from darkness to light, from the authority of Satan unto God. Before Paul was saved, he was under the authority of Satan. The Jewish religion was the authority of darkness through which Paul was controlled.

If we would have the proper understanding of Colossians 1:13, we need to consider this verse in the context of the whole Epistle. Considering the book as a whole, we see that the authority of darkness includes the Jewish religion with its observances, especially circumcision; it also includes Gentile ordinances, philosophy, mysticism, and asceticism. Throughout the world today people are under darkness, just as they were when the book of Colossians was written. To be in darkness is simply to be without light. Every university and every social group is under the authority of darkness. Every aspect of society, including Christianity, is in darkness. Do not think that darkness is found only where there is evil. Paul was telling the Colossians that God had delivered them out from under the authority of darkness, that is, out from legalities, ordinances, practices, asceticism, mysticism, and philosophy. Although these include the highest products of culture, they are nonetheless the authority of darkness by which Satan controls people.

We need to ask ourselves how much we are still under the authority of darkness. We may talk a lot about living Christ, but how much do we really live by Him? In our daily lives, many of us are still under some aspect of the satanic authority of darkness. Unconsciously, subconsciously, and spontaneously we live according to the self, not according to Christ. How much of each day do you live in the spirit and walk according to the spirit? How much time do you still live and walk in the self? Whenever we live in the self, we are under the control of the authority of darkness and are systematized by Satan. We are under Satan's control whenever we are in the natural man or live according to the self. Because of this satanic control, many have the sense that they are in darkness, that they have no light. The reason they are under darkness is that they are still controlled in some way by the authority of darkness. All of mankind, religious and nonreligious ones alike, are in darkness. In this darkness Satan's authority is exercised in various ways to systematize people and to control them.

Satan has many ways to control Christians. New ones who visit our meetings may be under the authority of darkness, especially the darkness of doctrine and of doctrinal understanding. Most Christians are under some form of doctrinal control. They are not aware that this control is the authority of darkness.

Others are under the authority of darkness because they live according to some natural virtue. They may be kind or humble in a natural way. However, even through virtues such as these, Satan may control us and hold us under the authority of darkness. Some do not receive light because they are under the darkness of their natural virtue. Every natural virtue is an aspect of the authority of darkness.

Many saints are controlled by their disposition, either by a quick disposition or by a slow one. Whatever our disposition may be, Satan can use it to control us.

When you read this word about the scope of the authority of darkness and about all the ways Satan uses to keep us in darkness and to control us, you may wonder how we should live. It may seem that we have no way to go on. Whatever we are, whatever we do, whatever we think, and whatever we say—all is under the authority of darkness. This is our actual situation. The only thing we can do is go to the cross and allow the cross to deal with every aspect of the satanic authority of darkness. The cross is our unique way.

We also must believe Paul's word in 1:13. We have already been delivered out of the authority of darkness.

II. TRANSFERRED INTO THE KINGDOM OF THE SON OF HIS LOVE

A. The Kingdom of the Son Being the Authority of Christ

We have been not only delivered out of the authority of darkness, but also transferred into the kingdom of the Son of God's love. The kingdom of the Son is the authority of Christ (Rev. 11:15; 12:10).

B. The Son of the Father Being the Expression of the Father as the Source of Life

The Son of the Father is the expression of the Father as the source of life (John 1:18, 4; 1 John 1:2). The Father as the source of life is expressed in the Son.

The Son of the Father's love is the object of the Father's love to be the embodiment of life to us in the divine love with the authority in resurrection. The Son, as the embodiment of the divine life, is the object of the Father's love. The divine life embodied in the Son is given to us in the divine love. Therefore, the object of the divine love becomes to us the embodiment of life in the divine love with the authority in resurrection. This is the kingdom of the Son of His love.

It is easier to give an illustration of the kingdom of the Son of His love than it is to give an adequate definition of it. Consider your experience. Coming to realize that the Lord Jesus is so loving and lovable, we began to love Him. As we love the Lord Jesus, we are conscious of a sweet sense of love. Not only does this sense of love include the Lord Jesus, but it also includes us. We realize that we also are the objects of the divine love. As objects of this divine love, we spontaneously come under a certain control or ruling. Before we began to love the Lord Jesus, we were free to do whatever we wanted. But the more we say, "Lord Jesus, I love You," the less freedom we have. Before we began to love the Lord Jesus, we did not sense this ruling or restriction. We could mistreat people or engage in worldly entertainments without any sense of inward restriction. But as those who love the Lord Jesus, we have come under His rule. This rule is not harsh; on the contrary, it is sweet and pleasant. Oh, we are restricted and ruled in such a sweet way! Because of the pleasantness of the Lord's rule in us, we do not care even to speak a vain word or to have a thought that is displeasing to Him. We are ruled and restricted to the uttermost in the sweetness of love. This is the kingdom of the Son of His love.

The more we are willing to be restricted and ruled by the Lord Jesus out of our love for Him, the more we shall grow in life, even in the abundance of life. This indicates that the kingdom of the Son of His love is for our enjoyment of Christ as life. Here we are freed from everything other than Christ, not only from evil things, but also from things such as philosophy, ordinances, observances, and asceticism. When we were holding to our philosophy, ethics, asceticism, and ordinances, we were under the authority of darkness. But God has delivered us out of this authority and has transferred us into a kingdom of love that is full of life and light. Here we have no observances, rituals, ordinances, practices, philosophies, mysticism, Gnosticism, or asceticism. We just have Christ, the Son of His love. Here we have love, light, and life. This is to live by Christ.

To live by Christ means that we do not live by anything other than Christ. If we see what it is to live by Christ, we shall realize that many of us are still under some form of control established by the self, a control set up and carried out by the self. This kind of control is the authority of darkness. If we are under this authority, we receive no light in reading the Bible, and we have no utterance in prayer. Although the Father has delivered us out of the authority of darkness, out of our natural thought, emotion, preference, and behavior, we may still remain in some aspect of our natural being. This causes us to be held under the authority of darkness. Because, in actuality, we are under the authority and control of darkness and are not in the kingdom of the

Son of His love in a practical way, we have little enjoyment of Christ as the portion of the saints.

I can testify that by the Lord's mercy I am not controlled by the darkness. Others may sometimes wonder why, in certain respects, I do not seem consistent. The reason is that I am not under the control of any aspect of darkness. Concerning matters that are not sinful, I am flexible and may give one answer at one time and a different answer at another time. Remember, the book of Colossians does not deal with sin, but with ordinances, practices, and philosophies. Suppose a brother asks me about eating a certain kind of thing. I may tell him that he has the liberty to eat whatever he desires. But to another brother asking the same question I may give a different answer, an answer appropriate to his situation. It may appear that I am not consistent. Actually, it is not a matter of consistency, but of refusing to be under the control of the authority of darkness through ordinances and observances.

To insist on a particular ordinance or practice is to be under the authority of darkness. Our Father has delivered us from the authority of darkness and transferred us into the kingdom of the Son of His love. Here we are restricted by the divine love in the divine life. Instead of ordinances, observances, religion, or isms, we have Christ and Christ alone. If we see this, there will be no disputes or divisions in the church life.

If we have anything divisive among us, that is an indication that some element of the authority of darkness is still with us. The division and confusion among Christians today are the result of the influence of the authority of darkness. If we have seen what it is to live by Christ, we shall not have observances or ordinances. This does not mean that we do not honor the holy Word. We believe and honor the Bible, but we do not take the Bible as a book of observances and ordinances. Instead, we take it as the revelation of the living Christ.

To be transferred into the kingdom of the Son of the Father's love is to be transferred into the Son who is life to us (1 John 5:12). The Son in resurrection (1 Pet. 1:3; Rom. 6:4-5) is now the life-giving Spirit (1 Cor. 15:45b). He rules us in His resurrection life with love. This is the kingdom of the Son of the Father's love. When we live by the Son as our life in resurrection, we are living in His kingdom, enjoying Him in the Father's love.

We have been transferred into a realm where we are ruled in love with life. Here, under the heavenly ruling and restriction, we have genuine freedom, the proper freedom in love, with life, and under light. This is what it means to be delivered out of the authority of darkness and transferred into the kingdom of the Son of His love. Here in this kingdom we enjoy Christ and have the church life. Here there is no opinion or division. Here we have one thing: the church life with Christ as everything to us. This is the revelation of the book of Colossians.

In Colossians the authority of darkness refers to the good aspects of culture and of our character, disposition, and natural being. The authority of darkness includes our virtues, religion, philosophy, observances, ordinances, principles, and ethical standards. God has delivered us out of all this and has transferred us into the kingdom of the Son of His love, where we live under a heavenly rule and restriction. In this kingdom we are not under a harsh rule, but under the loving rule of the Son. Here we do not sense that we are under righteousness, power, or authority, but under the loving and lovable Lord Jesus. The more we tell the Lord Jesus that we love Him, the more we are freed on the one hand, and the more we are restricted and ruled on the other hand. Because we love Him, we desire to take Him as our person and as our life. This is the proper Christian life for the church life.

LIFE-STUDY OF COLOSSIANS

MESSAGE FIVE

CHRIST—THE PREEMINENT AND ALL-INCLUSIVE ONE, THE CENTRALITY AND UNIVERSALITY OF GOD

Scripture Reading: Col. 1:15, 18; 3:11

THE BACKGROUND—THE AUTHORITY OF DARKNESS

In His dealings with the Jewish religionists, the Lord Jesus declared that they were blind (Matt. 15:14; 23:16,17, 19, 24, 26). In John 12:46 the Lord Jesus said, "I have come a light into the world, that every one who believes in Me may not remain in darkness." The Lord let the people know that without Him they were in darkness. Furthermore, in John 8:12 He declared, "I am the light of the world; he who follows Me shall by no means walk in darkness, but shall have the light of life." The Lord's word here indicates that anyone who does not receive Him as life will not have any light, but will walk in darkness.

The Gospels indicate clearly that the Jewish religion which was formed and constituted according to God's Word had become darkness. With this darkness there was an authority, the authority identified by Paul in Colossians 1:13 as the authority of darkness. The Pharisees and priests were under this authority of darkness. In fact, this satanic authority of darkness controlled all of Judaism; it controlled the temple, the priesthood, and even the understanding of the Scriptures. Judaism was altogether under the control of the authority of darkness. In the Gospels this darkness is related not to the Gentile world, but to the Jewish religion, to the religion formed according to the Scriptures.

Even more than the four Gospels, the book of Acts reveals that the Jewish religion had become altogether the authority of darkness under which people were controlled. The Jewish religionists were responsible for casting the apostles into prison and for killing Stephen. Saul of Tarsus was one of these religionists under the control of the authority of darkness. As he was carrying out the will of the authority of darkness through aggressively persecuting those who called on the name of the Lord Jesus, he was confronted by the Lord on the way to Damascus. As Paul testified later, he "saw in the way a light from heaven, above the brightness of the sun" shining round about him (Acts 26:13). Furthermore, the Lord spoke to him, saying, "Saul, Saul, why persecutest thou me?" (Acts 26:14). Through the shining of this light and the Lord's speaking, Saul of Tarsus was delivered out of the authority of darkness and was transferred into another realm, a realm of light, which is the kingdom of the Son of God's love.

According to the New Testament, the Son of God is the expression of the divine life and its embodiment. This means that the kingdom of the Son is a realm of life. The fact that the kingdom into which we have been transferred is the kingdom of the Son of God's love indicates that this realm of life is in love, not in fear. The kingdom in which we find ourselves today is a realm full of life, light, and love.

Just as the Jewish religion has become a part of the authority of darkness, so the church also has fallen under the prevailing authority of darkness. Degradation began to take place not long after the church had come into existence. In 1 Corinthians we see evil things such as division, fornication, and lawsuits. Colossians, on the contrary, deals not with sinful things, but with religion, observances, ordinances, and philosophy. Although the saints in Colosse did not fall into evil things, they did come under the authority of darkness by allowing the highest products of culture to invade the church.

As he was writing the Epistle to the Colossians, Paul seemed to be saying, "Dear saints at Colosse, before I believed in Christ, I spent years under the authority of darkness in Judaism. But one day I was delivered out of that authority and transferred into the kingdom of the Son of God's love. Through the preaching of the gospel, you also have been delivered out of the authority of darkness and transferred into the same wonderful realm that I am in. Why then have you gone back to the very things from which you have been delivered? You have returned to the Jewish religion and Greek philosophy. You have once again come under those concepts that used to control your thought and life in the past. This means you are now under the very authority of darkness from which you have been delivered. You have been carried off as a spoil, as a prey. Why do you still observe new moons, Sabbaths, and regulations concerning eating and drinking? Don't you know all that is the authority of darkness?" Paul knew that the saints in Colosse had again fallen under the satanic authority of darkness.

In the same principle, the Catholic Church, the Protestant denominations, and the various independent Christian groups are to a certain extent under the authority of darkness today. They are in darkness because for the most part they have Christ in name, but not in reality. Christ is the unique light. Apart from Him, there is no light. The reason so many Christians are in darkness is that they do not have Christ in an experiential way. Those in the seminaries may study theology and Christology, but they may not have the genuine experience of God and of Christ. Therefore, they are without light.

Many believers insist that the Bible is full of light. This, of course, is true. But if we do not read the Word in the Lord's presence, even our reading of the Scriptures will be in darkness. We shall be like the Pharisees addressed by the Lord Jesus in John 5:39 and 40: "You search the Scriptures, because you think that in them you have eternal life, and it is these that testify concerning Me; and you are not willing to come to Me that you may have life." It is possible to have the Bible in our hand and yet still be blind and in darkness. The religionists were offended when Christ told them they were blind (John 9:39-41). They thought they were in light because they had the Scriptures in an outward way. But actually they were blind because they did not have Christ, who alone is the light of the world. Any place where the Lord Jesus is not present is under the authority of darkness.

We need to apply this principle to ourselves. Any part of our being or of our daily life that is without Christ is in darkness. If we in the Lord's recovery do not have Christ experientially and in a practical way in our daily walk, we are in darkness. Do not think simply because you hear so many messages and teachings you are in the light. It is very possible that you are still in darkness.

For example, we may still be under the authority of darkness in our married life. When a brother is exchanging words with his wife, both he and his wife are in darkness. Because they are in darkness, they accuse and blame each other. The same is true when there are arguments between brothers or between sisters. Our experience testifies that whenever we live, walk, and behave in the self, we are in darkness. There is no need to commit some gross sin in order to be in darkness. Simply living according to the self puts us in darkness, for it causes us to be separated from Christ.

We should never think that darkness prevails only in Judaism, in Catholicism, or in the denominations and divisions, but not in us. It is possible that we ourselves may still be under the authority of darkness. Whenever we are in the natural man, not taking Christ as our person and living by Him, we are in darkness. We must remember that He alone is light. He must saturate and prevail in every aspect of our daily living. Otherwise, at least certain parts of our daily walk will not be filled with Christ, and those parts of our life will be in darkness.

Our homes have many rooms. Some rooms may be in the light, whereas others may be dark. The same may be true of our inner being and of our daily living. In certain respects, our life and our walk may be bright, full of light, because Christ occupies the prevailing position there. However, in other parts of our being or in other aspects of our living, we may be closed to the Lord and not allow Him to touch us. Those parts of our life and living that are closed off from Christ are spontaneously in darkness because Christ, the One who is the very light, has no place. Only when Christ occupies every part of us and every aspect of our daily walk can we be wholly in the light and altogether be delivered from the control of the authority of darkness.

The mistake the Colossians were making was that of receiving and following something other than Christ. To accept something in place of Christ is not only to be in darkness, but also to be under the controlling authority of darkness. Anything that is a substitute for Christ—philosophy, religion, character, virtues, concepts, opinions—becomes the authority of darkness to control us. At Colosse, the authority of darkness was Jewish religious observances, pagan ordinances, philosophy, mysticism, and asceticism. Although these things seemed to be good, they were actually the authority of darkness because they replaced Christ. They caused Christ, the light, to be set aside. Therefore, darkness became prevailing once again and controlled the saints in the church. This was the situation in Colosse, and may also be the situation today.

THE PREEMINENCE AND ALL-INCLUSIVENESS OF CHRIST

With this as the background, we need to see that Christ is the preeminent and all-inclusive One, the centrality and universality of God. The book of Colossians reveals that Christ is preeminent, that He has the first place in everything. Both in the first creation and in the new creation Christ occupies the first place. In 1:15 we are told that Christ is the "firstborn of all creation," and in 1:18, that He is the "firstborn from among the dead." The new creation of God is by resurrection. For Christ to be preeminent in the new creation means that He is the first in resurrection. He is the first both in creation and in resurrection. This means that He is the first in the old creation, the universe, and in the new creation, the church. The universe is the environment in which the church exists as the Body of Christ to express Christ in full. Christ is not only first in the church, the Body, but also first in the environment, the universe. This means that He is first in everything.

Colossians 1:19 says, "For in Him all the fullness was

pleased to dwell." What is the fullness spoken of in this verse? Many would answer that it is the fullness of the Godhead. Although this is correct, here Paul does not modify the word fullness by a phrase such as "of the Godhead" or "of God." He simply says that all the fullness was pleased, was happy, to dwell in Christ. There is something in this universe known as the fullness, and this fullness is pleased to dwell in the preeminent, all-inclusive Christ.

Many Christians fail to distinguish between the fullness and the riches. When they speak of the fullness of the Spirit, they mean the riches of the Spirit. In 1:19 fullness does not denote the riches of what God is, but the expression of those riches. All the expression of the rich being of God, both in creation and in the church, dwells in Christ. All creation and all the church are filled with Christ as such an expression of God's riches. Such a fullness is pleased with this. This is pleasant to Christ.

Fullness here means expression. If something has no fullness, it cannot be expressed. But if a thing has fullness, it can be expressed. For example, if I have very little love, my love cannot be expressed. But if my love is full, the fullness of my love will be its expression. In the same principle, the fullness is the expression of all that God is.

In 1:19 Paul speaks of the fullness as *the* fullness, using no word to modify it. This indicates that he is speaking of the unique fullness. To modify the fullness in any way would imply that it is not unique. In order to preserve the uniqueness of the fullness, Paul did not use a modifier. Hence, the fullness here is simply *the* fullness.

The fullness, the expression of God, is a person. Many of the personal pronouns in the verses following 1:19 refer to the fullness as a person. This indicates that the fullness is the expression of God, even God Himself. In this fullness the Son is preeminent, for all the fullness is pleased to dwell in Him. Therefore, He must have the first place in the environment and in the church. He is the preeminent One.

He is also the all-inclusive One. Christ is the reality of all the positive things in the universe. If we know the Bible and

God's economy, we shall realize that Christ is the heavens, the earth, the sun, life, light, the star, trees, flowers, water, air, and food. The material things are pictures of what He is to us. Furthermore, Christ is all the divine attributes, such as power, holiness, righteousness, kindness, and love. He is also the human virtues, such as humility and patience. Moreover, He is the church and every member of the church, God's building and every stone in the building. This means that Christ is you and me.

Some twist our words and falsely accuse us of teaching pantheism. Pantheism is the satanic belief that identifies God with the universe. This is devilish, and we repudiate it without reservation. But according to the revelation of the Bible, we must testify that Christ, the all-inclusive One, is the reality of all positive things. When we say that Christ is you and me, we do not mean that we are God or that we shall ever become God. Likewise, when we say that Christ is the real food (see John 6:55), we do not mean that physical food is God. Such a concept is not only absurd, but also satanic. Those who accuse us of teaching pantheism have never seen the all-inclusiveness of Christ.

As the all-inclusive One, Christ is the centrality and universality of God. This expression was first used by Brother Nee in 1934, at the third overcomer conference held in Shanghai. He pointed out from the book of Colossians that the all-inclusive Christ is the center and the circumference of God's purpose. Christ is both the centrality and universality of God's purpose. He is the hub and also the rim. In other words, Christ is all. Again I say that this is not pantheism. It is simply a statement of the fact that Christ is both the center and the circumference of God's economy.

When I first heard Brother Nee speak of the centrality and universality of Christ, I was greatly surprised. Never before had I heard such a thing. From my experience in the years since 1934 I can testify that Christ truly is the center and the circumference, the centrality and universality of God's economy. In God's economy Christ is everything.

The saints in Colosse were wrong in turning to religion

and philosophy. Such things are against God's economy, where there is room only for Christ, the One who is all and in all.

I. CHRIST IN THE GOSPELS

A. Incarnated to Put On the Old Creation

Let us now, in the way of an overall survey, look at Christ in the Gospels, in the Acts, in the Epistles, in Revelation, and then in Colossians. In the Gospels we see that Christ was incarnated to put on the old creation. John 1:14 says that the Word became flesh. Flesh here denotes man of the old creation. Strictly speaking, God did not create the flesh; He created a body for man. But through the fall, sin entered into man's body and caused it to become flesh. Hence, the flesh in John 1:14 refers to man as part of the old creation. Man, the head of creation, had become flesh. By incarnation Christ became a man and thereby put on the old creation.

B. Passing through Human Living to Express God

Throughout His human living, Christ expressed God. John 1:18 says that no one has ever seen God, but the Son has declared Him. During the thirty-three and a half years of His life on earth, Christ declared God and expressed Him.

C. Crucified to Terminate the Old Creation

When Christ was crucified, He terminated the old creation. If a Jew were asked what happened when Jesus was crucified, he would probably answer that a man named Jesus of Nazareth died on the cross. A new Christian may say that it was his Savior who was crucified. A more advanced Christian may reply that not only was Christ crucified as his Savior, but that he himself also was crucified with Christ. An even more advanced Christian may answer that Christ, the self, Satan, and the world were all dealt with on the cross. However, not even this answer is sufficient. On the cross, Christ crucified sin, Satan, the world, the old man, and the entire creation. Moreover, the law of commandments in ordinances was also crucified there.

Therefore, the death of Christ terminated the entire old creation.

D. Resurrected to Produce the Church, the New Creation

According to the Gospels, Christ was resurrected to produce the church, the new creation. He was the one grain of wheat that fell into the ground and produced many grains in resurrection to form the church (John 12:24).

II. CHRIST IN THE ACTS

In the Acts we see that Christ has been exalted to be the Head over all things to the church. Acts also reveals that after His exaltation Christ descended as the Spirit to carry out God's intention. Furthermore, the book of Acts reveals that Christ has been propagated to bring the church into existence.

III. CHRIST IN THE EPISTLES

In the Epistles we see that Christ is our righteousness (1 Cor. 1:30), our life (1 John 5:12), our life supply (Phil. 1:19), our holiness (1 Cor. 1:30), our redemption (1 Cor. 1:30), and our glory (1 Tim. 1:1). All these aspects of Christ indicate that we shall experience a full transformation resulting in glorification.

IV. CHRIST IN REVELATION

In the book of Revelation we see that Christ is the testimony of the churches. In the churches we testify only to Christ. Furthermore, in Revelation we see that Christ is the King in the coming kingdom and, ultimately, the center of the New Jerusalem in eternity.

V. CHRIST IN THE BOOK OF COLOSSIANS

We have seen that in the book of Colossians Christ is the preeminent One (1:15, 18) and the all-inclusive One (3:11). He is the centrality and universality of God's economy. In Colossians Paul uses a number of unique expressions to describe Christ, expressions that are not found elsewhere in the Scriptures. This indicates that in Colossians we have the highest revelation of Christ found in the Bible. This book is like Mount Zion, the highest peak among the mountains. We appreciate this book because, in a unique way, it presents Christ as the preeminent and all-inclusive One, the centrality and universality of God.

LIFE-STUDY OF COLOSSIANS

MESSAGE SIX

CHRIST—THE PORTION OF THE SAINTS

Scripture Reading: Col. 1:12-14; Gen. 12:2b, 3b, 7; Gal. 3:14

In this message we shall consider Christ as the portion of the saints. In 1:12 Paul says, "Giving thanks to the Father, Who qualified you for a share of the portion of the saints in the light." As we shall see, the portion of the saints is the all-inclusive Christ for our enjoyment.

THE PROMISE OF THE LAND

According to the book of Genesis, no promises were given that involved blessing or enjoyment before the call of Abraham. Of course, in Genesis 3:15 there is the promise that the seed of the woman would crush the head of the serpent. This promise, however, does not involve a promise of blessing or enjoyment. In chapters four through eleven of Genesis there is no record of such a promise. A promise of blessing is first mentioned in Genesis 12, at the time God called Abraham out of his country and his father's house. Here the Lord specifically mentions the land (Gen. 12:1).

We may be familiar with the story of Abraham and assume that we understand everything related to it. As we read of God's calling of Abraham and of the promises made to him, we may take things for granted. Thus, when we read about the land, we may have no impression of its significance. However, if we read the Word carefully, we shall surely realize that God's promise to Abraham concerning the land is striking and very important. This promise made in Genesis is a seed that grows and develops throughout the Old Testament. In a very real sense, apart from the first eleven chapters of Genesis, the entire Old Testament is a story about the land of Canaan. The subject of the Old Testament is this good land, the land flowing with milk and honey. Nevertheless, few Christians pay adequate attention to this.

When I was with the Brethren, I was encouraged to study typology and prophecy. However, three important matters were not brought to my attention, and I received no help with respect to them. These three matters were God's creation of man in His own image, after His likeness, and with His dominion; the tree of life, the river with the precious materials, and the bride built from Adam's rib; and the promise of the good land. Only after I had been a Christian for years did I begin to focus my attention on these things. Those familiar with my messages realize that, in one way or other, they deal with these three things.

God's promise to Abraham with respect to the good land is of great significance. When Paul was writing the Epistle to the Colossians and was speaking of the portion of the saints, he no doubt had in mind the picture of the allotting of the good land to the children of Israel in the Old Testament. The Greek word rendered portion in 1:12 can be also rendered lot. Paul used this term with the Old Testament record of the land as the background. God gave His chosen people, the children of Israel, the good land for their inheritance and enjoyment. The land meant everything to them. In fact, the question of the land is a serious issue in the Middle East even today. The problem in the Middle East regarding Israel and the surrounding nations is a problem of the land.

THE SEED AND THE LAND

The promise to Adam and Eve in Genesis 3 was the promise of the seed of the woman. But the promise God made to Abraham was not only that of the seed, but also that of the land. The seed promised in Genesis 3:15 becomes the land in Genesis 12. When the children of Israel entered into the land of Canaan, they inherited not only the seed, but also the land. We may interpret the seed both as a person and also as a seed sown into soil. This means that Christ is not only a descendant, but a seed sown into the land. Christ is both the seed and the land.

In Colossians do we have Christ as the seed or the land? In this book Christ is both the seed and the land. Colossians 2:7 says that we have been rooted in Christ. This indicates that He is the land. But in 3:4 we are told that Christ is our life. This indicates that He is also the seed. However, in Colossians Christ is revealed more as the land than as the seed. Christ is our portion, our lot, our everything, just as the land was all things to the children of Israel. The land provided whatever the children of Israel needed: milk, honey, water, cattle, grain, minerals. In writing this Epistle, Paul employed the concept of the all-inclusive land in order to charge the misled Colossians not to take anything other than Christ Himself. Anything that is not Christ is related to the authority of darkness, and we should not accept it. Rather, we should simply remain in the good land and not allow any foreign element to come in. Christ alone is our portion, and we should accept only what is of Him.

THE SPIRIT BEING THE GOOD LAND

Before Paul wrote Colossians, he wrote the Epistle to the Galatians. In Galatians 3:14 he says, "That the blessing of Abraham might come on the Gentiles through Jesus Christ; that we might receive the promise of the Spirit through faith." Some Christian teachers believe that the blessing of Abraham refers to justification by faith. According to the context, however, this blessing must refer to the good land. In Genesis 12 the blessing God promised to give Abraham was the land. In Galatians 3:14 Paul links the blessing of Abraham to the promise of the Spirit. This indicates that the promise of Abraham, the promise of the good land, is the Spirit. Hence, the Spirit is the good land.

In Galatians 3:14 Paul speaks of the Spirit. This should remind us of John 7:39. This verse says, "The Spirit was not yet, because Jesus was not yet glorified." The Spirit in Galatians 3:14 and John 7:39 is the ultimate expression of the Triune God. The Spirit is a unique term which denotes the processed God. The Father is the source. The Son of God as the course was incarnated, lived on earth, was crucified, and on the third day was resurrected. Incarnation, crucifixion, and resurrection are all aspects of a process. In resurrection, Christ, the last Adam, became the life-giving Spirit (1 Cor. 15:45). According to John 1:14, the Word, who was God, became flesh. According to 1 Corinthians 15:45, the last Adam, who is Christ, became the life-giving Spirit. Many Christian teachers argue that the life-giving Spirit in this verse is not the Holy Spirit. To believe this is to believe that there are two Spirits who can give life, the Holy Spirit and the life-giving Spirit. The life-giving Spirit is no doubt the very Holy Spirit who gives life. This Spirit is the ultimate consummation of the processed God. This Spirit is nothing less than the all-inclusive Christ. As the good land is an all-inclusive type of Christ, and as Christ has become the Spirit, so the Spirit, the all-inclusive Spirit as the processed God, is eventually the good land to us, the New Testament believers, as a fulfillment of God's promise to Abraham that all the nations of the earth would be blessed in him (Gen. 12:3).

According to Galatians 3:14, the promise is the promise of the Spirit. But Galatians 3:16 says that the promises were made to Abraham's seed, which is Christ. It is difficult to reconcile these verses. On the one hand, the Spirit is the all-inclusive Christ. On the other hand, this promise, this Spirit, was given to Christ as the seed. Although this is difficult to explain doctrinally, it is rather easy to understand according to experience. When we believed in the Lord Jesus, we received Him as the seed, as life. However, this seed is the all-inclusive, life-giving Spirit, the reality of the good land. This means that the very Christ whom we received as the seed is the Spirit typified by the good land. Christ came into us as the seed. But as we live by Him, He becomes the land which is our portion.

DELIVERED OUT OF THE AUTHORITY OF DARKNESS AND TRANSFERRED INTO THE ALL-INCLUSIVE CHRIST

Just as the good land was the portion of the children of Israel, so Christ today is the portion of the saints. We have pointed out that as Paul was composing 1:12 he had in mind the type of the land of Canaan. In 1:13 he goes on to say, "Who delivered us out of the authority of darkness and transferred us into the kingdom of the Son of His love." This verse reminds us of the way the children of Israel were delivered out of Egypt and transferred into the good land. Thus, Paul's concept in 1:13 is the same as that revealed in the exodus from Egypt and in the entering into the good land. In ancient times, God delivered His people out of Egypt and brought them into the good land. God the Father has done the same thing with us. He has delivered us out of the authority of darkness, typified by Pharaoh and Egypt, and has transferred us into the all-inclusive Christ, typified by the good land. Just as the children of Israel were transferred out of Egypt into a land flowing with milk and honey, a land where there was no tyranny, so we have been transferred into a marvelous realm, called the kingdom of the Son of the Father's love. Therefore, to be qualified for a share of the portion of the saints is actually to enter into the good land. Paul's composition of 1:12 and 13 is thus according to the picture in the Old Testament.

THE PASSOVER, THE MANNA, AND THE LAND

In writing 1 Corinthians Paul also used pictures from the Old Testament. In 1 Corinthians 5:7 we see that Christ is the Passover, and in 10:3 and 4, that He is the manna. According to the pictures in the Old Testament, it was by the passover lamb that the children of Israel were delivered from Egypt, and it was by the manna that they were sustained in the wilderness. The tabernacle erected in the wilderness typifies the movable church life. This kind of church life is not solid or well established. After the children of Israel had entered into the good land and had enjoyed the blessing promised to Abraham, they built the temple with stone, by the unsearchably rich supply of the good land. The temple typifies the solid church life. In 1 Corinthians we have the church typified by the tabernacle, but in Colossians and Ephesians, the church typified by the temple. The

Christ we enjoy in Colossians is not simply the lamb and the manna, but the good land, the lot, the portion of the saints.

Many Christian teachers speak about the passover, the manna, and the tabernacle. But I doubt that any have seen that the good land is a type of the all-inclusive Christ. This type of Christ can be fulfilled only by the Spirit. Christians may know the Spirit of God, but they may not know the Spirit, the all-inclusive, life-giving Spirit as the ultimate expression of the processed Triune God as the fulfillment of the promise of the good land. For us, the good land promised by God to Abraham is the Spirit. In other words, the Spirit is the blessing God promised to Abraham.

WALKING IN SPIRIT

In Galatians 5:16 Paul charges us to walk in spirit. The spirit should be our realm, the sphere, in which we walk. Furthermore, in Galatians 5:25 Paul says, "If we live in the Spirit, let us also walk in spirit" (Gk.). This indicates that the Spirit is our good land. The Christ revealed in the New Testament, especially in Colossians, is the all-inclusive land. This land is Christ as the all-inclusive Spirit. Hallelujah, we have received a share in such a portion!

THE NEED FOR AN EXODUS

If we see this, we shall not allow things other than Christ to invade the church. The Colossians were troubled by ordinances, practices, philosophy, and asceticism because they did not see that Christ as the all-inclusive Spirit was their portion, their good land. In place of this portion, they accepted observances, ordinances, and philosophy. In principle, the same is true of today's Christianity. Christianity has been invaded by culture. Not one part of Christianity has been exempt from this. All of Christianity has been flooded by culture. The purpose of the Lord's recovery is to bring us out of all this to Christ Himself. At first, the world was Egypt. Now the religion of Christianity has become an Egypt where God's people are held in bondage. The Lord's people today need an exodus. Many of us can testify that when we came into the church life, we made an exodus and were delivered out of the authority of darkness.

ONLY CHRIST

When the children of Israel were wandering in the wilderness, they remembered the flavor of the leeks, onions, and garlic they enjoyed in Egypt, and they still longed to eat that kind of food. But when the children of Israel entered into the good land, nothing with an Egyptian flavor was brought into Canaan. That would have been blasphemous to God. To bring into the church something other than Christ is also a blasphemy. In the good land there are no Egyptian leeks, onions, and garlic. In the good land we enjoy only the produce of the land. In the same principle, there is no worldly "garlic" in the church life, only Christ as the portion of the saints. If we see this, we shall be kept from bringing any foreign element into the Body of Christ.

We have seen that the portion of the saints is Christ as the good land, the all-inclusive Christ as the life-giving Spirit. Firstly, Christ is the seed that gives us life. Then He becomes the kingdom, the realm, the sphere, in which we live and walk. Therefore, Christ is our seed and our land, our life and our realm. This is Christ as the portion of the saints.

LIFE-STUDY OF COLOSSIANS

MESSAGE SEVEN

PARTAKING OF CHRIST IN THE LIGHT

Scripture Reading: Col. 1:12-13; Gen. 1:3; Psa. 36:9; 119:105; Isa. 2:5; Matt. 4:16; John 1:4; Acts 26:18; 1 John 1:5; Rev. 21:23

In 1:12 Paul says that the Father has qualified us "for a share of the portion of the saints in the light." Many may read this verse without paying attention to the phrase "in the light." Christ, our portion, is to be enjoyed by us in the light. In this message we need to consider what it is to partake of Christ, the portion of the saints, in the light.

The Bible reveals that when God restored the universe He had judged because of the rebellion of Satan, the first thing He did was to cause light to appear. Darkness had been on the surface of the deep. Then God said, "Let there be light," and light came forth (Gen. 1:3). This took place on the first day. On the fourth day we see a more solid form of light: the sun, the moon, and the stars. The light on the first day was rather abstract and unsubstantial, but on the fourth day we have the solid luminaries. By this we see that the re-creation of the universe, or its restoration, was carried out by light.

References to light abound in the Old Testament. Psalm 36:9 says, "In thy light shall we see light." In Psalm 119:105 the psalmist declares, "Thy word is a lamp unto my feet, and a light unto my path." Furthermore, Isaiah 2:5 says, "O house of Jacob, come ye, and let us walk in the light of the Lord."

Although the Bible has much to say about light, it is difficult to give an adequate definition of light. Light is real and substantial, yet it is mysterious. Nevertheless, the Bible indicates that light was a basic factor in the restoration of the universe and that light is necessary for God's people to walk in His presence.

Matthew 4:16 says that when Jesus was walking through Galilee, the "people sitting in darkness saw a great light, and to those sitting in the region and shadow of death, to them light sprang up." In John 8:12 the Lord Jesus said that He is the light of the world and that whoever follows Him will not walk in darkness, but have the light of life. However, if we do not follow Him as the light, we shall be in darkness. Furthermore, at the time of Paul's conversion, the Lord Jesus told him to open the eyes of people so that they may turn from darkness to light (Acts 26:18). This indicates that unbelievers, whether Jews or Gentiles, are in darkness. Anyone who does not believe in the Lord Jesus is in darkness and needs to turn from darkness to light. Furthermore, 1 John 1:5 says that God is light and that in Him there is no darkness. If we say that we have fellowship with Him and yet walk in darkness, we lie. Since God is light, if we have fellowship with Him, we also shall be in the light.

I. THE LIGHT

The Bible reveals that the light is related to God, the Word of God, Christ, the life of Christ, the believers, and the church.

A. God

We have pointed out that 1 John 1:5 says that God is light. He alone is the source of light. The Word of God, Christ, the life of Christ, the believers, and the church can all be light because they have God as their source.

B. The Word of God

Psalm 119:105 says that the Word of God is a lamp to our feet and a light to our path, and 119:130 says that the entrance of God's words gives light. The Word of God is light because it contains God. If the Bible did not contain God, the words of the Bible could not enlighten us. The source of the Bible is God, and God is light. Therefore, the words of the Bible are the shining of light.

C. Christ

In John 9:5 the Lord Jesus said, "While I am in the world, I am the light of the world." God and Christ are one. Since God is light, Christ also is light. Christ is the light of the world in a very definite way. The world in John 9:5 denotes society, mankind. Thus, Christ is the light not just in a general way, but in a definite way as the light of society, of mankind.

D. The Life of Christ

The life of Christ is also light. John 1:4 says, "In Him was life, and the life was the light of men." When we receive Christ as life, this life becomes light in us, shining upon us and enlightening us from within.

E. The Believers

Those who believe in Christ are also the light. Speaking of the believers, the Lord Jesus said, "You are the light of the world" (Matt. 5:14). In Philippians 2:15 Paul says that the believers "shine as lights in the world." The Greek for lights is better rendered luminaries. A luminary does not have light in itself; it reflects light that comes from another source. The believers are luminaries. In ourselves we have no light. The light comes from the oil, the Spirit, burning within us. The source of our light is not ourselves, but Christ as the Spirit.

F. The Church

In Revelation 1:20 we see that the church is a lampstand, a stand that holds and supports a burning lamp. The lamp is Christ with God in Him as light (Rev. 21:23). In the universe there is one light, God Himself. The Triune God is the unique light.

II. PARTAKING OF CHRIST IN THE LIGHT

Colossians 1:12 indicates that we partake of Christ as the portion of the saints in the light. Since God alone is light, we must turn to God and be in His presence in order to partake of Christ. We have been called into the marvelous light of God (1 Pet. 2:9). Before we were saved, we were altogether in darkness. Everything related to us and our human situation was in darkness. When the gospel came to us, it came with light. This caused us to repent to God. As we repented, we spontaneously opened to Him. At the time we repented and were saved, we experienced something shining within us. We believed in the Lord Jesus and thanked Him for dying on our behalf, and we received Him as our Savior and Lord. In this way, the inner shining was intensified. Therefore, at the time of our conversion, light entered into us. Many of us can testify that in the days following our conversion we experienced such a light. In that light Christ became our portion. Although we did not have this kind of knowledge at the time, we did have this experience.

However, after we were saved, we were distracted from this inner shining. Many of us were encouraged by diligent Christian workers to pay attention to doctrine and Bible teaching. Hence, instead of remaining in the presence of the Lord and treasuring the inner shining, we turned to good things that are not Christ Himself. We exchanged the presence of Christ for doctrine, for some type of observance or practice, and thereby lost the inner shining. The result was that once again we were in darkness. Before we were saved, we were in the horrible darkness of the world. But after we were saved, we were in the darkness of teachings, observances, works, formalities, and religious rituals. Some of these things may be good, but they are not Christ Himself. Having been distracted from God as the light, we lost the enjoyment of Christ as our portion.

In more than fifty years of contacting Christians, it has been hard to find any who speak of the enjoyment of Christ. Do you know of Christians who testify of Christ as their portion and who encourage others to partake of Christ and to enjoy Him? When I was young, I was taught to follow Christ and to walk in His steps. I was also charged to worship Him as the Lord and Master in the heavens. But I was never told that I could enjoy Christ. I was not taught that Christ is my life supply and the portion for my enjoyment.

When we were saved, we had a sense of the sweetness of Christ. Deep within, we realized how enjoyable Christ is. Then through the help of pastors, ministers, and Christian workers, many of us were distracted and led away from the enjoyment of Christ. We turned from the inner sense of the sweetness of Christ to religious duty. This brought us into darkness again, and the inward shining ceased. Many of us spent years in this condition. But one day, out of desperation, we laid aside our religious duty, turned to the Lord, and cried out to Him. We asked Him what had happened to us. By turning to the Lord, we turned once more from darkness to light. Then, in the light, we again began to enjoy Christ as the portion of the saints.

The only way to partake of Christ and to enjoy Him is in the light. God and Christ are light. When we turn to the Lord and come into His presence, we are in the light and spontaneously begin to enjoy Him as our portion.

All Christians should read the Bible. However, it is possible to be in darkness even when we are reading the holy Word. We may read the Scriptures without being in the presence of the Lord. If we do this, the more we study the Bible, the more we shall be in darkness, removed from the Lord's presence. The proper way to read the Scriptures is not only with the mind, but also with our seeking spirit, looking to the Lord's countenance as we read. By pray-reading the Word we are brought into the Lord's presence in this way. When we read the Bible in a pray-reading spirit, opening ourselves to the Lord, we are brought into His presence. Spontaneously we are in the light, and Christ becomes our portion.

No matter what kind of disposition we may have, we have one weakness in common: we all like to argue. But whenever we argue, we are brought into darkness. Because we are not in the light, we cannot enjoy Christ as our portion. After arguing, we need to repent and make a thorough confession to the Lord. Through repentance and confession we are brought back to the light and to Christ as our portion.

If we are in darkness because of arguing with someone, we cannot enjoy Christ. We may come to the meetings, but we have no enjoyment of Christ, because we are not in the light. Christ cannot be our portion in darkness. He can only be our passover. However, even for Christ to be our passover requires that we repent and confess. If we would enjoy Christ as our portion, we cannot stay in Egypt in darkness, but must turn wholly to God.

Because I have found that arguing puts me in darkness, I cannot bear to argue. Time after time, I am forced to stop speaking because of the threat of darkness. I pray to the Lord and ask Him to forgive me for expressing the self. Through such repentance and confession the light returns and I am able to continue to enjoy Christ.

Light is the presence of God. If we would be in light, we must turn to Him from within. Then His presence will become the shining light. In this way Christ becomes the portion of the saints in a practical way.

If we would fellowship with God, we must walk in the light (1 John 1:7). In many things we may be able to pretend, but in this matter of enjoying Christ in the light there is no room for pretense. You may deceive others, but you cannot deceive the Lord. He is too real, genuine, honest, and practical.

In Isaiah 2:5 the prophet sounded forth a call, "O house of Jacob, come ye and let us walk in the light of the Lord." During Isaiah's time, the children of Israel were occupied with their religion, but they had lost the light of the Lord because their heart had turned from Him. They had the temple, the priesthood, and the sacrifices. But because they had turned their heart away from God, they were in darkness. They were not walking in the light. Therefore, Isaiah called them to come and walk in the light of the Lord. This was a call to repent and to confess in order to be brought into the Lord's presence.

Psalm 36:8 and 9 describe a person who has returned to the Lord and who is in the Lord's presence. Such a one is satisfied with the fatness of God's house and drinks of the river of the Lord's pleasures. He knows the Lord as the fountain of life, and in the light of the Lord he sees light. In this light the portion of the saints becomes his enjoyment. We need to abide in Christ and walk in the light of life (John 8:12) that we may partake of Christ in the light (Eph. 5:14).

We need to have more and more contact with the Lord. We need to read His Word with an unveiled face and an open heart. As we fellowship with the Lord and follow the inner anointing, we shall experience Him as the life within us in a practical way. This life is the light. If we follow the inner anointing, we shall be in light. We are also brought into the light by fellowshipping with others in a genuine way. In fellowship there is the shining of light. Moreover, we need to be in the church life and attend the meetings, for in the church and in the meetings we are in the light. In the meetings of the church we often have the sense deep within that we are in the light enjoying Christ as our portion. All these are means by which we may be in the light to enjoy Christ as the portion of the saints.

Now we can understand why after Paul speaks of light in Colossians 1:12, he goes on in the next verse to speak of the authority of darkness. It seems as if Paul was telling the Colossians, "You have been delivered out of the authority of darkness. But now you have gone back into darkness. You have lost the very light into which you had been transferred." We have pointed out that in Colossians the authority of darkness includes observances, ordinances, philosophy, and the various isms. Through the influence of these things, the Colossians were carried off as a prey, just as the children of Israel were carried away from the good land into Babylon. In a sense, many Christians today have been carried away from the kingdom of the Son of God's love, away from the realm of light, the sphere of light. As a result, they have lost the enjoyment of Christ as the portion of the saints.

III. THE LIGHT OF LIFE BEING THE REALM OF LIFE

Light is a realm, a sphere. The realm of light is a realm of life. This means that the light of life is the sphere, the realm, of life. This realm of life and light is the kingdom of the Son of the Father's love. Light rules by its enlightening. Hence, when the light of life shines and rules, it is a kingdom. When we are in the light, we are in the realm of life, in the kingdom of the Son of the Father's love. This kingdom is in contrast to the authority of darkness, which is the kingdom of Satan. The New Jerusalem will be the ultimate consummation of the realm of life. The whole city will be a realm of life, full of light. This realm will be the light of life.

Darkness is dissipated by light (Gen. 1:2-3; Rev. 21:24; 22:5). When light comes, darkness is scattered.

If you pray-read the verses we have covered in this message, you will learn how to be in the light enjoying Christ as the portion of the saints in your practical experience. May we all practice to enter into the light where we enjoy Christ as the portion of the saints.

LIFE STUDY OF COLOSSIANS

MESSAGE EIGHT

CHRIST—THE FIRSTBORN OF ALL CREATION

Scripture Reading: Col. 1:15-17; Rev. 3:14

In this message we shall consider what it means for Christ to be the firstborn of all creation (1:15-17). The main purpose of the book of Colossians is to show that Christ is everything, that He is all. In the universe everything that exists is included under one of two basic headings: the Creator and the creation. In order to show us that Christ is all, the Bible tells us that Christ is both the Creator and the firstborn of all creation. If He were only the Creator but not the firstborn of creation, then He would not be all.

THE HERESY OF ANGEL WORSHIP

In Colossians Paul deals with such things as Jewish observances, Gentile ordinances, mysticism, Gnosticism, and asceticism. Of all the negative things that he deals with, one stands out as especially serious—the worship of angels, which is a form of idolatry. To worship anything other than God, including such creatures as angels, is idolatry. Nevertheless, because they regarded themselves and others as being unworthy to contact God directly, certain heretical teachers in Colosse advocated angel worship. They taught that God is very high and that we are very low, that God is glorious and that man is corrupt. Therefore, according to their heretical teaching, we could not be worthy to contact God directly. According to them, we must have some kind of intermediary. These teachers said that the angels are the intermediaries between us and God. This was the concept behind the angel worship that had invaded the church in Colosse.

The angel worship Paul dealt with in this Epistle was related to a sense of humility. Some thought it was a sign of humility to believe that they were not worthy to worship God directly. Apparently they had some ground in the Bible for their position. The Bible records that the law was not given to Moses by God directly; it was given through the mediation of angels (Gal. 3:19). Hence, in the giving of the law the angels functioned as intermediaries. The heretical teachers went on to say that the angels should be the intermediaries between God and fallen man. They encouraged the saints to show humility by following this way of worship. It seems as if these teachers were telling those in Colosse, "You shouldn't be so proud as to think that you can go directly to God. You must humble yourselves and recognize your need of angels to serve as intermediaries between you and God." Paul was fighting against such a concept when he said, "Let no one purposely defraud you of your prize, in humility and worship of the angels" (2:18). We should not be carried away by someone's humility or by a teaching regarding angel worship.

THE HEAD OF ALL RULE AND AUTHORITY

In 2:9 and 10 Paul says, "For in Him dwells all the fullness of the Godhead bodily, and you in Him are made full, Who is the Head of all rule and authority." The words rule and authority refer to the angels. Christ is the Head of all the angels, not only of subordinate angels, but of those angels that have rule, power, and authority.

We need to see why Paul inserts the phrase in 2:10, "Who is the Head of all rule and authority." It is rather easy for us to understand that all the fullness of the Godhead dwells in Christ bodily, that is, in bodily form (2:9). When Christ was on earth, He had a physical body, and in that body all the fullness of the Godhead dwelt. Because the fullness dwells in Him and because we are in Him, it follows that in Him we are made full (2:10). But then Paul suddenly speaks of Christ being the Head of all rule and authority. The One in whom all the fullness of the Godhead dwells and the One in whom we are made full is the very Head of all rule and authority. It is crucial that we see the significance of this.

In order to understand the insertion of this clause, we need to consider it in the context of the whole book. Colossians reveals that Christ is all. Paul emphasized this to the Colossians because they had accepted the heresy of angel worship. Apparently the saints in Colosse did not think that Christ could be the intermediary between them and God. To their concept, Christ was too exalted to help them in this way. Hence, they felt they needed angels as intermediaries. This was the reason Paul told them that Christ is the Head of all angels. As long as we have Christ, who is everything, there is no need for us to rely on angels. If we need an intermediary, Christ is our intermediary. This is not the function of angels. Yes, God is high, and we are very low. But this does not mean that we need angels as intermediaries. In Christ we have been made full; we are short of nothing. Because the Colossians were regarding angels as intermediaries, they needed to see that Christ is the Head of all the angels. Christ is everything. As long as they had Him, they had been made full. Both doctrinally and experientially, we should be able to testify that in Christ we have been made full and are short of nothing. In Christ we have God, righteousness, life, and all the positive things in the whole universe. By having Christ we have the One who is the Head of all angels. How mistaken the Colossians were in accepting the heresy of angel worship! Because Christ is all, we should go to Him for everything we need. Now we see that Paul added a clause in 2:10 in order to impress the Colossians with the fact that we do not need angels as intermediaries because our Christ is the Head of all rule and authority. He is the Head of all angels.

Colossians reveals that Christ is everything, both the Creator and the firstborn of all creation. If Christ were only the Creator but not anything of the creation, He would not be all. Thus, the fullness, the expression of the Triune God, would not be complete. Paul's concept in Colossians is profound. The fullness, the full expression of the Triune God, dwells in Christ. As the One who is all, He is both the Creator and the firstborn of all creation. This is a basic principle.

THE IMAGE OF THE INVISIBLE GOD

Colossians 1:15 says that Christ is the "image of the invisible God." Then, in the very same verse, Paul says that Christ is the "firstborn of all creation." Why does he put these two matters together, the image of the invisible God and the firstborn of all creation? God is invisible. But the Son of His love, "the effulgence of His glory and the express image of His substance" (Heb. 1:3), is His image, expressing what He is. The image here does not mean a physical form, but an expression of God's being in all His attributes and virtues. This interpretation is confirmed by Colossians 3:10 and 2 Corinthians 3:18.

To say that Christ, the all-inclusive One, is the image of God implies that He is the very God, the Creator. When we see Christ, we see the expression of the invisible God, for He Himself is God. If I had written the Epistle to the Colossians, I would have said simply that Christ is God the Creator. Paul, however, did not write in such a simple way. He said that Christ is the image of the invisible God, God Himself expressed.

FIRST AMONG ALL CREATURES

In 1:15 Paul goes on to say that Christ is the firstborn of all creation. This means that in creation Christ is the first. Christ as God is the Creator. However, as man, sharing the created blood and flesh (Heb. 2:14), He is part of the creation. "Firstborn of all creation" refers to Christ's preeminence in all creation, since from this verse through verse 18 the apostle stresses the first place of Christ in all things. This verse reveals that Christ is not only the Creator, but also the first among all created things, the first among all creatures.

Some insist that Christ is only the Creator, not a creature. But the Bible reveals that Christ is both the Creator and a creature, for He is both God and man. As God, Christ is the Creator, but as man, He is a creature. How could He have flesh, blood, and bones if He were not a creature? Did not Christ become a man? Did He not take on a body with flesh, blood, and bones? Certainly He did. Those who oppose this teaching are short of knowledge. Actually, they are heretical, because they do not believe that Christ truly became a man. Rather, they believe only that He is God, and such a belief is heresy. Our Christ is God, has always been God, and always will be God. But through incarnation He became a man. Otherwise He could not have been arrested, tried, and crucified; and He could not have shed His blood on the cross for our sins. Praise the Lord for the truth that our Christ is both God and man!

As God, Christ is eternal and did not need to be born. But in 1:15 He is called the firstborn of all creation. Anything that requires birth must be a creature, part of creation. If Christ were only God and not man, He could not have been born, for God is infinite and eternal, without beginning or ending. But as a man, Christ had to be born. Hallelujah, Christ was born as a man! Isaiah 9:6 says, "For unto us a child is born, unto us a son is given...and his name shall be called The mighty God, The everlasting Father...." As the child born to us, Christ is called the mighty God. As the Son given to us, His name is called the eternal Father. As the mighty God and the eternal Father, Christ is eternal. But as the child and a son, He had to be born. Some argue that Christ was born, but not created. According to the Bible, birth is the carrying out of creation. Therefore, to be born is to be created.

NO TIME ELEMENT WITH GOD

Some may wonder how Christ could be the firstborn of all creation since He was born less than two thousand years ago, not at the very beginning of creation. If we would understand this properly, we need to realize that with God there is no time element. For example, according to our estimate of time, Christ was crucified about two thousand years ago. But Revelation 13:8 says that Christ was slain from the foundation of the world. Both are right. However, God's reckoning is much more important than ours. In the eyes of God, Christ was crucified from the foundation of the world. In eternity, God foresaw the fall of man. Therefore, also in eternity, He made preparation for the accomplishment of redemption.

The difference between God's estimate of time and ours also helps us understand why Christ is called the second man (1 Cor. 15:47). From our point of view, the second man was Cain, the son of the first Adam. But from God's point of view, the second man is Christ.

We may apply this matter of the different ways of reckoning time to Christ as the firstborn of all creation. According to our sense of time, Christ was born in Bethlehem approximately two thousand years ago. But in the eyes of God, the Lord Jesus was born before the foundation of the world. If He was slain from the foundation of the world, certainly He must have been born before then. Therefore, according to God's perspective in eternity, Christ was born in eternity past. This is the reason that, according to God's viewpoint, Christ has always been the first of all creatures. God foresaw the day that Christ would be born in a manger in Bethlehem. Because Christ is the first among the creatures, we can say that as the all-inclusive One He is both the Creator and part of creation.

FAITHFUL TO THE TRUTH

In a previous message I pointed out that in 1934 Brother Nee gave a series of messages in Shanghai on the centrality and universality of Christ. At Brother Nee's request, I polished my notes of these messages and prepared them to be printed in Brother Nee's paper called *The Present Testimony.* When this material was translated into English, the translator took the liberty of interpreting Brother Nee's concept regarding Christ as the first of the creatures in a way to which Brother Nee would never have agreed. Instead of saying, as Brother Nee did, that "the Son is the number one of the creatures," the translator says that "the Son is the head of all creation." Surely this is not a faithful translation, but an interpretation according to the concept of the translator.

Brother Nee had the boldness to say just what the Bible says. During that conference in 1934 we read from Brother Nee's Chinese translation of Colossians 1. In this translation he made it very definite that Christ is the first of all creatures. This is an example of Brother Nee's boldness for the truth. He did not care for what men say; he cared only for what the Bible says. Nevertheless, the translator of these messages changed Brother Nee's words in order to avoid trouble with certain theological concepts. This is not faithful to Brother Nee's ministry.

If we care for the truth, we shall testify that Christ, the image of the invisible God, the very Creator, as the firstborn of all creation, is the first among all creatures. In this sense, Christ is not only the Creator, but also part of creation.

IN HIM, THROUGH HIM, AND UNTO HIM

Colossians 1:16 says, "Because in Him were all things created in the heavens and on the earth, the visible and the invisible, whether thrones or lordships or rulers or authorities; all things have been created through Him and unto Him." "In Him" means in the power of Christ's Person. All things were created in the power of what Christ is. All creation bears the characteristics of Christ's intrinsic power. (See note on this verse in Darby's *New Translation.)* "Through Him" indicates that Christ is the active instrument through which the creation of all things was processed. Finally, "unto Him" indicates that Christ is the end of all creation. All things were created for His possession.

BEFORE ALL THINGS

In verse 17 Paul goes on to say, "And He is before all things." This indicates His eternal preexistence.

ALL THINGS SUBSISTING IN HIM

Moreover, verse 17 says that "all things subsist together in Him." For all things to subsist together in Christ means that they exist together by Christ as the holding center, just as the spokes of a wheel are held together by the hub at their center.

LIFE-STUDY OF COLOSSIANS

MESSAGE NINE

CHRIST—FIRSTBORN FROM AMONG THE DEAD

Scripture Reading: Col. 1:18-23

We have seen that the book of Colossians reveals that Christ is everything. In the universe there is God the Creator, and there is the creation. According to 1:15, Christ is the image of the invisible God. This means that He is nothing less than God Himself in full expression. Furthermore, Christ is the firstborn of creation, the first among all God's creatures.

God has accomplished two creations, the old creation and the new creation. The old creation includes heaven, earth, mankind, and millions of different items. The new creation is the church, the Body of Christ. Verses 15 through 17 unveil Christ as the first in the original creation, as the One who has the preeminence among all creatures. Verse 18 shows that Christ is the first in resurrection as the Head of the Body. He is the One who has the first place in the church.

The first creation came into being through the speaking of God. In the words of Romans 4:17, God called the things not being as being. The new creation, on the contrary, came into being through resurrection, through the death and resurrection of the old creation. In this new creation, the church, Christ is the firstborn from among the dead.

THE TWO BIRTHS OF CHRIST

As the Son of God, Christ has passed through two births. The first birth took place at His incarnation, and the second, in His resurrection. All Christians realize that Christ was born through incarnation, but not many regard His resurrection also as a birth. Acts 13:33 indicates that Christ was begotten, or born, in resurrection. Through resurrection He was begotten as the Son of God. However, before His incarnation, in eternity, He was already the Son of God. Why then did He need to be born the Son of God in resurrection? Before His incarnation, Christ was not a man. He was simply the infinite, eternal God. But in the fullness of time, Christ was conceived by the Holy Spirit in the womb of Mary, and nine months later He was born in a manger in Bethlehem. According to John 1:14, the Word who is Christ became flesh. This means that He took the step of becoming a man. How marvelous that through incarnation the infinite, eternal God became a man! However, in becoming man, He did not cease to be God.

After living on earth for thirty-three and a half years, Christ was crucified. Then in resurrection He took a second step to be born the second time and become the firstborn Son of God. Before His resurrection, Christ was the only begotten Son of God (John 3:16). But through resurrection the only begotten Son became the firstborn among many brothers (Rom. 8:29). According to Hebrews 2:10, God is leading many sons into glory. These many sons are the many brothers of Christ as the firstborn Son.

Through the two births of Christ, divinity has been brought into humanity, and humanity has been brought into divinity. By the incarnation of Christ God was brought into man. Prior to Christ's incarnation, God was outside of man. However, through Christ's incarnation God was brought into humanity. We may say that with the birth of Christ God was born into man. Therefore, by Christ's first birth in incarnation God was brought into man and became one with man. Then through Christ's resurrection man was brought into God. When the Lord Jesus was on earth, God was living in a man, for God was in Him. Now, through Christ's resurrection, man has been brought into God. Hallelujah, as a man Christ is in the heavens! God has been brought into man, and man has been brought into God. What a transaction! What marvelous two-way traffic! In this two-way traffic God came into man through incarnation, and man was brought into God through resurrection.

Have you ever heard that Christ, the Son of God, has passed through two births? You may have heard that you needed a second birth, the birth in the spirit through the Holy Spirit, but not that Christ was born twice, first in incarnation and then in resurrection. In eternity Christ was God. Through His incarnation He became a man, and through resurrection He became the firstborn Son of God.

OUR EXPERIENCE OF CHRIST'S TWO BIRTHS

Through Christ, God has been brought into us, and we have been brought into God. Praise Him for such a mingling! When we were born again, simultaneously Christ was born into us, and we were brought into God. Therefore, in our Christian life we have an inward and personal experience of both of the births of Christ. With Christ, His birth in resurrection came thirty-three and a half years after His birth through incarnation. However, in our experience of Christ, God was brought into us and we were brought into God at the same time. Praise the Lord for the marvelous traffic between God and us!

Colossians 1:19 says that all the fullness was pleased to dwell in Christ, and 2:9 declares that in Christ dwells all the fullness of the Godhead bodily. In 2:10 Paul goes on to say that in Christ we are made full. Because all the fullness dwells in Christ and because we have been put into Christ, we have been made full, filled with the divine riches. Hallelujah, in Christ we are made full! In a very real sense, we who believe in Christ are complex, for we are in the One who is very complex. If He were not complex, there would have been no disputes regarding His Person.

THE ALL-INCLUSIVE ONE

Christology is the theological study of the Person of Christ. Some teach the truth that Christ is both God and man. Others, however, teach that Christ is God, but not man or that He is man, but not God. There is no need for disputes concerning the Person of Christ. He is all-inclusive. He is God, man, and the reality of every positive thing in the universe. If we see that Christ is everything, we shall not argue about Him. A number of verses indicate clearly that Christ is God. For example, Romans 9:5 speaks of "Christ, Who is over all, God blessed forever." At a certain time Christ became a man. Then through death and resurrection He became the firstborn Son of God.

In His life on earth, the Lord Jesus was among His disciples, but He was not in them. Hence, it was necessary for Him to pass through death and resurrection in order to come into His disciples as the life-giving Spirit (1 Cor. 15:45), the Spirit of reality (John 14:17). In John 14 through 16 the disciples were troubled by the fact that the Lord was leaving them. It seems that He was telling them, "If I do not go, there will be no way for Me to come into you. I must pass through death and resurrection in order to become the life-giving Spirit. Then I shall be in you forever." On the day of His resurrection, the Lord appeared to the disciples, breathed into them, and said, "Receive the Holy Spirit" (John 20:22). This is the Spirit promised in 14:16-17, 26; 15:26 and 16:7, 13. The Lord's breathing of the Holy Spirit into the disciples was the fulfillment of His promise of the Holy Spirit as the Comforter. By breathing the Spirit, the holy breath, the life-giving Spirit, into the disciples, the Lord imparted Himself into them as life and every positive thing.

As the Son of God, Christ took two extraordinary steps. Firstly, He took the step of incarnation to become a man for the accomplishment of redemption and for the termination of the old creation. Secondly, in resurrection He became the life-giving Spirit in order to regenerate us to produce the church, God's new creation.

THE PREEMINENT ONE

In both the old creation and the new creation Christ is the first and occupies the first place, the place of preeminence. Both in the universe and in the church, Christ is the preeminent One. If we see this as a vision, not as a mere doctrine, our living and our church life will be revolutionized. We shall realize that in all things Christ must be the first.

In 1:18 Paul says, "That He might have the first place in all things." In the Bible to be the first is to be all. Since Christ is the first both in the universe and in the church, He must be all things in the universe and the church. As the first, He is all.

God's way of reckoning in this matter is different from ours. According to our estimation, if Christ is the first, then something else should be the second, third, and others in sequence. However, from God's point of view, for Christ to be the first means that He is all.

The first Adam included not only Adam as an individual, but all of mankind. In the same principle, in the eyes of God, the firstborn of the Egyptians included all the Egyptians. The firstborn includes all. Therefore, for Christ to be the firstborn in the universe means that He is everything in the universe. In like manner, for Christ to be the firstborn in resurrection means that He is everything in resurrection. For Christ to be the firstborn both of the old creation and of the new creation means that He is everything both in the old creation and in the new creation. This corresponds to Paul's word in 3:11, where he says that in the new man, in the new creation, "There cannot be Greek and Jew, circumcision and uncircumcision, barbarian, Scythian, slave, freeman, but Christ is all and in all." In the new man Christ is everyone and in everyone. In the new creation there is room only for Christ.

HAVING THE ONE WHO IS ALL

In this Epistle Paul seemed to be telling the Colossians, "Why are you so foolish? You have received Christ, the One who is everything. He is the first in the old creation and in the new creation. What need is there for you to take in something else? Why do you worship angels and turn to Gnostic philosophy? Why do you follow the elements of the world? Don't you know that the very Christ you have received and now possess is everything? He is the Head of all the angels, and you are in Him. In Him you have been made full."

Chapters two and three reveal that the Colossians had turned to various isms—Gnosticism, mysticism, legalism, and asceticism. These isms are the elements of the world. Because we have the all-inclusive Christ, we do not need isms. We do not need philosophies, theories, and practices, for we have the One who is all in all. Christ is profound. What philosophy can equal Him? All the treasures of wisdom and knowledge are hidden in Him (2:3).

This Christ is the image of God, the full expression of God. He is not the hidden God, the concealed, mysterious God; He is God expressed, the image of the invisible God. Furthermore, He is the first among God's creation. As we have pointed out, this indicates that He is everything. He is the alpha, the omega, and all the letters in between (Rev. 22:13). He is everything in the universe, and He is the first in the new creation, the church.

INFUSED AND SATURATED

Perhaps you are wondering how this understanding of Christ can help you in a practical way. If for a period of thirty days you are occupied with the revelation of Christ in Colossians, you will be revolutionized, reconstituted, and transformed. Pray over these messages on Colossians and have fellowship concerning them, and you will see what a difference it will make in you. I can testify that it makes a tremendous difference when the vision of the all-inclusiveness of Christ pervades our being. When you see this vision, you will hate everything that issues from the self. You will despise not only your hatred, but even your love, kindness, and patience. As this vision causes you to hate the self, it will constrain you to love the Lord. You will say, "Lord Jesus, I love You because You are everything. Lord, there is no need for me to struggle or strive to do anything. O Lord, You are so much to me. You are God, You are the firstborn of all creation, and You are the firstborn from among the dead." I suggest that you pray-read Colossians for thirty days. Pray until all the aspects of Christ revealed in this book saturate your being. We do not need regulations or teachings—we need to be infused and saturated with Christ as the all-inclusive One.

If Christ is infused into you, you will drop everything that is not Christ, and you will be constituted with Christ in your very being. Religion gives people doctrines and teaches them how to behave. The book of Colossians, on the contrary, speaks of the all-inclusive Christ. This Christ is already in us, but we need to see Him, know Him, be filled with Him, be saturated with Him, and become absolutely one with Him.

THE FULL ENJOYMENT OF CHRIST

In Him we are made full. We may be familiar with these words in 2:10, but, sorry to say, we may take them for granted. Have you seen that in Christ you are made full? I doubt that many see the reality of this verse. We may know this as a doctrine, but not as an experience. In our actual living, we may not yet be full. Thus far, our partaking of the unsearchable riches of Christ has been very limited. Christ is our good land, but we do not yet enjoy Him in full as this land. Paul's purpose in Colossians is to bring us into the full enjoyment of Christ as the all-inclusive land.

ALL THINGS RECONCILED TO GOD

In 1:20 Paul goes on to say, "And through Him to reconcile all things to Him, making peace through the blood of His cross—through Him, whether things on the earth or things in the heavens." "Through Him" means through Christ as the active instrument through which the reconciliation was processed. To reconcile all things to God is to make peace with God for all things. This was accomplished through the blood of the cross of Christ.

Not only the things on the earth but also things in the heavens needed to be reconciled to God. This indicates that things in the heavens also are not right with God due to the rebellion of Satan, the archangel, and the angels who followed him. His rebellion has contaminated the heavens.

Verse 21 says, "And you, who once were alienated and enemies in your mind by evil works." Because we were sinners, we needed redemption. Because we were also enemies of God, we needed reconciliation to Him. Our enmity toward God was mainly in our corrupted mind.

In the body of His flesh Christ has reconciled us to God in order to present us holy, blameless, and without reproach before God (v. 22). However, we still need to "continue in the faith, grounded and steadfast and not moved away from the hope of the gospel" (v. 23). The faith here does not denote the act of believing, but the object of our belief.

Here Paul speaks of the hope of the gospel. Christ in us is the hope of glory (v. 27), from whom we should not be moved away.

LIFE-STUDY OF COLOSSIANS

MESSAGE TEN

CHRIST'S RELATIONSHIP TO CREATION

Scripture Reading: Col. 1:15-19

THE MEANS OF CREATION

In the traditional teaching prevailing in Christianity, Christ is considered to be the Creator. Although as God Christ is the Creator, no verse in the Bible says explicitly that Christ created the heavens, the earth, and all the things in the universe. When some hear this, they may wonder about John 1:3. This verse says, "All things came into being through Him, and apart from Him nothing came into being which has come into being." This verse does not say that Christ created all things. It says that all things came into existence through Christ. The King James Version of this verse says, "All things were made by him." This, however, is not an accurate translation. The Greek preposition should be rendered through and not by. Hence, this verse does not say that all things were created by Christ, but that all things came into existence through Christ. This indicates that Christ is the means of creation.

Some may think that Hebrews 1:10-12 says that Christ is the Creator. However, these verses are a quotation from Psalm 102 that indicates that God is the Creator. Here they are quoted to prove that Christ is God.

Christ is in fact the Creator of all things. But the point we are emphasizing here is that the Bible does not say specifically that Christ is the Creator. Rather, the Bible speaks of Christ as the means of creation, as the means through which all things came into being. If we speak of creation in a general sense, it is correct to say that Christ is the Creator. But if we wish to speak more definitely, it is better to say that Christ is the means of creation.

Colossians 1:16 says, "In Him were all things created." The King James Version says, "By him were all things created." This rendering is not accurate. The Greek preposition used here is more accurately translated by the English word in. To say that all things were created in Christ indicates that He is the means of the creation of all things. However, if this verse is rendered, "By him were all things created," it will say that Christ is the Creator, not the means of creation.

CHRIST EXPRESSING GOD IN CREATION

In 1:15 Paul says that Christ is the image of the invisible God. This means that Christ is the expression of the unseen God. At this point we need to ask in what way Christ expresses God. The answer is that He expresses God in creation. However, Christ does not express God in creation simply by creating all things in an objective way. If Christ were merely an objective Creator, not the subjective means of creation, Christ could not express God in creation. Keep in mind that all things were created not by Christ, but through Christ. This points to a process that took place in Christ.

In his note on Colossians 1:16 in his *New Translation,* J. N. Darby says that the words "in Him" mean in the power of Christ's Person. As Darby says, "He was the one whose intrinsic power characterized the creation." Commenting on the meaning of the Greek preposition used in the phrase "in Him were all things created," Darby says that it is "used generally for the character in which a thing is done" (*Collected Writings,* Vol. 33, p. 87). He also states that the "creation of all things was characterized and wrought by the inherent power which is in the Lord Jesus Christ, and all things subsist together as one ordered and law-governed whole by the same constant and inherent power" (*Collected Writings,* Vol. 31, p. 188).

Christ is the active instrument through which creation was processed. In this process God's power is expressed; it is made manifest. This is revealed clearly in Romans 1:20.

This verse says that the "invisible things of Him from the creation of the world, being apprehended by the things made, are clearly seen, both His eternal power and divine nature." In all created things God's power is made manifest. Hence, in Darby's words, creation bears the characteristics of Christ's intrinsic power.

SUBJECTIVELY RELATED TO CREATION

Christ is related to creation in a subjective way. Christ did not create the universe merely in an objective way as an objective Creator. He did not, so to speak, stand apart and call everything into being. On the contrary, the process of creation took place in Him, that is, in the power of His Person. Christ is the unique power in the universe. His very Person is this power. Therefore, creation was processed in Him. This means that He was not simply an objective Creator, but also the subjective instrument through which creation was processed. For this reason, creation bears the characteristics of Christ's intrinsic power. Instead of saying that Christ created the universe, the Bible says that all things came into being through Him or were created in Him. The words "by Him" are objective, whereas the words "through Him" and "in Him" are subjective.

The use of gasoline as the source of power in an automobile may be a helpful illustration. An automobile is operated by the driver, but it receives its power supply from gasoline. Since gasoline provides the power, an automobile bears the characteristics of the power of gasoline. But gasoline does not supply an automobile as an objective power; it empowers it subjectively by operating within certain mechanical parts of the automobile. If the power of gasoline were objective, an automobile would not bear the characteristics of the intrinsic power of gasoline. But since gasoline is subjectively related to the automobile, the vehicle driven by it bears the characteristics of its intrinsic power.

The King James Version of Colossians 1:16 says that all things have been created for Him. It is better to render the Greek "unto Him." "For Him" is objective, but "unto Him" is subjective. All things have been created in Christ, through Christ, and, ultimately, unto Christ. These expressions indicate that Christ has a subjective relationship to creation. Creation is not simply for Him; it is also unto Him. This means that it consummates in Him. The three prepositions in, through, and unto were used by Paul to point out the subjective relationship of Christ to creation. Creation took place in the power of Christ's Person, through Him as the active instrument, and unto Him as its consummation. Such a relationship is altogether subjective. Because of His subjective relationship to creation, Christ expresses God in creation. Creation expresses the characteristics of Christ who is the image of the invisible God.

ALL THINGS SUBSISTING IN CHRIST

In verse 17 Paul goes on to say, "All things subsist together in Him." This means that all things exist together by Christ as the holding center. For creation to subsist in Christ is a further indication that Christ is subjectively related to creation.

It is important to differentiate between the words exist, consist, and subsist. Colossians 1:17 does not say that all things exist in Christ or consist in Him; it says that all things subsist in Him. To exist is to be, to consist is to be composed or constituted, and to subsist is to hold together for existence. Imagine a wheel with its rim, spokes, and hub. All the spokes subsist together in the hub. The only way for the spokes to subsist is to be held together at the hub in the center of the wheel. This illustrates Christ's relationship to creation with respect to the fact that all things subsist in Himself.

We have pointed out that all things came into being in Christ, through Christ, and unto Christ. Nothing should be regarded as separate from Him. All things were made in the intrinsic power of Christ's Person, through Him as the active instrument, and unto Him as the consummate goal. Furthermore, all things subsist, are held together, in Him as the hub. Because all things were created in Christ, through Christ, and unto Christ and because all things subsist in

Christ, God can be expressed in creation through Christ who is the image of the invisible God.

ALL THE FULLNESS

In 1:19 Paul says, "For in Him all the fullness was pleased to dwell." The fullness here is virtually the equivalent of the image in verse 15. The image of the invisible God is the full expression of the unseen God. For the fullness to dwell in Christ means that all the expression of God, all of His image, was pleased to dwell in Him.

Verses 15 through 19 make up one section of the Epistle to the Colossians. In this section Christ is revealed as the first both in the old creation and in the new creation. As the One who is first in both of God's creations, Christ is the expression of God. God is expressed in Him because all things have come into being in Him, through Him, and unto Him, and they subsist in Him. This is true not only of the old creation, but even the more of the new creation. The new creation, the church, is Christ's Body, of which He is the Head. Through His subjective relationship to creation, Christ is the fullness of the unseen God, the image of the invisible God. The fullness in verse 19 is not a thing; it is a person who is the expression, the image, of the Triune God.

In verses 20 through 22, it is difficult to determine to whom the various pronouns refer. Verses 19 and 20 say that in Christ the fullness was pleased to dwell, and "through Him to reconcile all things to Him." If the fullness were not a person, how could it be pleased to dwell in Christ? The fact that the fullness can be pleased indicates that it is a person. The fullness was pleased not only to dwell in Christ, but through Him to reconcile all things to Him. In verses 19 and 20 two infinitives—to dwell and to reconcile—are joined by a conjunction. Hence, the fullness was pleased to dwell and to reconcile. The phrase "through Him" is used twice in verse 20. Both times it refers to Christ as the active instrument through which reconciliation was processed. But what is the antecedent of the pronoun Him, to whom all things are reconciled? The antecedent is the fullness spoken of in verse 19. This is the reason that in his *New Translation,* J. N. Darby uses the pronouns itself and it, in verses 20 and 22, to refer to the fullness in verse 19. The Greek pronouns, however, should not be regarded as neuter, but as masculine. This means that instead of saying "it," we should say "him." Therefore, all things have been reconciled to the fullness. In verses 21 and 22, we who were enemies have been reconciled by the fullness in the body of flesh through death so that we may be presented holy and blameless and without reproach before the fullness. How meaningful is this understanding of the passage! It is the fullness that dwells in Christ, it is the fullness that reconciles us, and it is to the fullness that we shall be presented. This fullness is God Himself expressed. This fullness was pleased to dwell in Christ, to reconcile us, and to present us to Himself.

THE EXPRESSION OF GOD IN ALL HIS RICH BEING

The Christ revealed in Colossians is all-inclusive. He is not only God, but also the firstborn of creation. All things came into being in Him and through Him. Furthermore, all things are unto Him and subsist in Him. Therefore, through Him is expressed all that God is. We have seen that all the fullness in verse 19 does not denote the riches of what God is, but the expression of those riches. The full expression of God in all His rich being, both in creation and in the church, dwells in Christ. The rich being of God is expressed both in the old creation and in the new creation through Christ as the One in whom, through whom, and unto whom all things came into being and as the One in whom all things subsist. It is in such a way that the invisible God is expressed.

When we consider the universe and the church, the old creation and the new creation, we see all the fullness of the Triune God. We behold the expression of the Triune God. This fullness was pleased to dwell in the Son and to reconcile all things to Himself for His expression. Furthermore, this fullness will present us holy, blameless, and without reproach to Himself so that He may have His expression in the new creation.

THE SON OF THE FATHER'S LOVE BEING THE IMAGE OF THE INVISIBLE GOD

Colossians 1:15 says, "Who is the image of the invisible God, firstborn of all creation." The relative pronoun who refers to the Son of God's love (v. 13). This means that the Son of the Father's love is the image of the invisible God. In verse 15 Paul puts the phrase "firstborn of all creation" in apposition to the phrase "the image of the invisible God." Grammatically this indicates that these expressions are synonymous. The image of the invisible God is the firstborn of all creation. The fact that verse 16 begins with the word because indicates that it gives the reason Paul said that the image of God is the firstborn of all creation. The reason is that "in Him were all things created in the heavens and on the earth, the visible and the invisible, whether thrones or lordships or rulers or authorities; all things have been created through Him and unto Him." Why is the image of the invisible God the firstborn of all creation? He is the firstborn because all things were created in Him, through Him, and unto Him.

We have seen that as the image of God Christ is the expression of God. If a person had no physical form or image, he could not be expressed. A person is expressed through his physical image. Although God is invisible, He is expressed through His image, which is His Son. The Son of the Father's love is the expression of the invisible God. This expression is firstly the firstborn of all creation, because all things were created in Him, through Him, and unto Him. The creation that came into existence through Him expresses God's eternal power and divine nature. Both the divine nature and the eternal power are the expression of the invisible God. If you study the universe in a thoughtful way, you will confess that it testifies of the eternal power and of the divine nature. Even many scientists realize that in creation some kind of extraordinary power exists. This power is Christ as the image of the invisible God.

The three prepositions used in verse 16—in, through, and unto—indicate that creation is subjectively related to

Christ. There is a subjective relationship between creation and Christ because of the process of creation and because of the goal, the consummation, of creation. In Christ and through Christ creation came into being. This indicates that creation is subjectively related to Christ because of the process by which it came into existence. Moreover, all of creation is unto Christ. This indicates that creation is subjectively related to Christ as the consummation, the goal, of its existence. Both in the process of creation and in the goal of creation Christ is expressed. Therefore, creation cannot be separated from Christ as the image of the invisible God.

CHRIST AS CREATOR AND AS THE MEANS OF CREATION

Christ is both God and Christ. As God He is the Creator, but as Christ He is God's anointed One and appointed One. As God's anointed and appointed One, Christ carries out God's commission. As God Christ is the Creator, but as Christ He is the instrument, the means, of creation. Therefore, in John 1:3, the emphasis is not that Christ is the Creator, but that He is the means through which creation was processed and came into existence. The same is true of Colossians 1:16. The process of creation was carried out in Him, through Him, and unto Him. He is the means, the instrument, through which and in which creation came into existence.

HOW CHRIST, THE IMAGE OF GOD, EXPRESSES GOD

Verses 16 through 18 are a definition of verse 15. The items found in these verses are related to Christ as the image of the invisible God. This means that Christ as the image of God is related to the process and goal of creation, to the firstborn of creation, to the subsistence of creation, and to the firstborn from among the dead. The issue of these items is all the fullness, the fullness in the old creation and the fullness in the new creation, spoken of in verse 19. Hence, the fullness in verse 19 is the image in verse 15.

How does Christ, the image of the invisible God, express God? As the Son of the Father's love, He expresses the Triune God because He is the One through whom both the old creation and the new creation came into being. Furthermore, He expresses the Triune God because He is the firstborn of both creations. This makes Him the full expression of God. All the fullness in verse 19 denotes the very Person of Christ. This is the reason that in the following verse Paul uses a masculine pronoun to refer to the fullness.

Praise the Lord that Christ is all-inclusive! In Paul's words in Colossians, Christ is the image of the invisible God, the firstborn of all creation, and the firstborn from among the dead. As the Son of the Father's love, He is the full expression of God, seen both in the old creation and in the new creation. As God, Christ has no beginning. But as the firstborn of creation, He had a beginning. Let us set aside the natural concept, believe the pure Word of God, and praise the Lord that as the all-inclusive One He is the full expression of the Triune God.

LIFE-STUDY OF COLOSSIANS

MESSAGE ELEVEN

THE STEWARDSHIP OF GOD

Scripture Reading: Col. 1:24-26

In 1:25 Paul says that he "became a minister according to the stewardship of God." For the sake of the full expression of God, there is the need for the stewardship of God.

It is important to understand accurately the meaning of stewardship. The Greek word rendered stewardship here, *oikonomia*, is the same word rendered dispensation in Ephesians 1:10 and 3:9. The word also appears in Ephesians 3:2, where Paul speaks of the stewardship of grace which had been given to him. According to ancient usage, *oikonomia* denoted a stewardship, a dispensation, or an administration. At the time of Paul, many rich families had stewards whose responsibility was to distribute food and other supplies to members of the household. Our Father has a great family, a divine household. Because our Father has such vast riches, there is the need in His household for many stewards to dispense these riches to His children. This dispensing is the stewardship. Hence, a stewardship is a dispensation.

The word dispensation here does not denote an age or means by which God deals with people; it refers to God's dispensing of His riches into His chosen ones. This dispensation is the stewardship with the dispensing ministry of the ministers of God. This ministry of dispensing is also God's administration. Today God administrates by dispensing Himself into us. This stewardship, this dispensation, this administration, is God's economy. In the New Testament economy of God there is the desperate need of the stewardship of God.

We have pointed out that stewardship refers to the dispensation of wealth in a royal or upper-class family. God's royal family is rich in Christ. According to the Epistle to the Colossians, God's family is especially rich in Christ as the all-inclusive and preeminent One, as the One who is the image of the invisible God, the firstborn of all creation, and the first-born from among the dead. The riches of such a Christ, who is the full expression of the Triune God, need to be dispensed into the members of God's family. This service of dispensing, which in 1:25 is called the stewardship of God, was the work of the Apostle Paul. It also should be our work today.

Not many ministers or workers in today's Christianity carry out the stewardship of God. This means that not many are actually dispensing the riches of Christ into the members of God's royal family. The stewardship of God is needed for this rich, all-inclusive, preeminent Christ to be dispensed into the members of His Body.

This stewardship is the ministry in the New Testament. The New Testament ministry is the dispensing of the unsearchable riches of the all-inclusive Christ into the members of God's family. The Apostle Paul dispensed the riches of Christ into the saints. This is what we are doing in the ministry today.

The stewardship of God is according to the economy of God. With God it is a matter of economy; with us it is a matter of stewardship. All the saints, no matter how insignificant they may seem to be, have a ministry according to God's economy. This means that every saint can dispense the riches of Christ into others.

The desire of God's heart is to dispense Himself into man. This is the central point of the whole Bible. God's economy is to carry out the dispensing of Himself into man. We share in this economy through our stewardship, our ministry of dispensing the riches of Christ. After the riches of Christ have been dispensed into us, we need to take up the burden to dispense them into others. With God these riches are His economy; with us they are the stewardship; and when they are dispensed by us into others, they become God's dispensation. When God's economy reaches us, it becomes our stewardship. When we carry out our stewardship by dispensing Christ into others, it becomes the dispensation of God into them. Hence, we have the economy, the stewardship, and the dispensation.

Those who bear responsibility in the local churches need to share in the stewardship of God. This means that the elders should be those who take the lead to dispense the riches of Christ into others. Although Christ is all-inclusive and preeminent, there is still the need for Him to be dispensed into the members of God's family. This dispensation takes place through the stewardship. Hence, between the unsearchably rich Christ and the members of His Body, there is the need of the stewardship. All those who take the lead in the Lord's recovery and have responsibility for the care of the churches need to realize that they have a part in such a divine stewardship. We are not here to carry on an ordinary Christian work. For instance, we are not concerned merely with teaching the Bible in an outward way. Rather, we desire to serve the riches of Christ to all the members of God's family. In our conversation with one another, we need to minister the riches of Christ. Even when we are invited to the homes of the saints for dinner, we need to dispense the riches of Christ. This is the stewardship of God.

Every member of the Body of Christ has a part in this stewardship. In Ephesians 3:8 Paul refers to himself as "less than the least of all saints." This indicates that Paul was even smaller than we are. If Paul could be a steward, then we also can be stewards and dispense the riches of Christ into others. In preaching the gospel, for example, we should not be concerned merely with winning souls. Rather, we should preach the gospel to carry out the stewardship of dispensing the riches of Christ into others. Day by day we need to fulfill our stewardship by dispensing the Triune God into man. Praise the Lord that we all have a share in this stewardship! We all have the privilege of dispensing the unsearchable riches of Christ into others. Therefore, we should not merely preach the gospel or teach the Bible; we should also impart the riches of Christ to others.

We have many opportunities to minister the riches of Christ to the saints. Suppose we are helping a family to move. We should not simply move the furniture, but we should supply the riches of Christ to the members of the family, especially to the sister. If we help in the moving without dispensing the riches of Christ, we may actually make things difficult for others. Our intention in helping a family move their belongings should be to dispense the riches of Christ. All our activity with respect to such a service should be with Christ.

Another opportunity to minister the riches of Christ to others is in giving or receiving hospitality. Both the hosts and the guests should minister the riches of Christ.

May the Lord open our eyes to see that we all have part in the stewardship of God. In every aspect of the practical church life, even in such things as ushering and cleaning the meeting hall, we need to dispense Christ into others. Firstly, we need to be filled with Christ and then minister the riches of Christ to others. This is our stewardship.

I. THE STEWARD'S SUFFERINGS

In 1:24 Paul says, "Now I rejoice in my sufferings on your behalf, and fill up that which is lacking of the afflictions of Christ in my flesh for His Body, which is the church." The afflictions of Christ are of two categories: those for accomplishing redemption, which have been completed by Christ Himself; and those for producing and building the church, which need to be filled up by the apostles and the believers.

The fact that Paul mentions the afflictions of Christ in connection with the stewardship of God indicates that the stewardship can be carried out only through suffering. If we desire to share in the stewardship of God, we must be prepared to suffer. All those who participate in the service of the church or in the ministry must be ready to partake of the afflictions of a steward. This means that we must be willing to pay whatever price is necessary to fulfill our stewardship.

We have pointed out that when we give or receive hospitality, we need to carry out our stewardship by dispensing the riches of Christ into others. However, to provide hospitality may involve a kind of suffering. In like manner, to be the guest in someone's home also may be a cause of suffering. I have been a guest in the homes of many saints. The hosts have invariably taken care of me in a marvelous way, doing everything necessary to meet my needs. Nevertheless, I suffered simply because I was not in my own home. No matter how adequate the hospitality may be, I am always glad to be back home. However, I am happy to testify that many have spoken of the nourishment, edification, and strengthening they have received through sharing in hospitality, as either a host or a guest. This indicates that to carry out the stewardship of God by dispensing the riches of Christ into the members of God's royal family is worth any kind of suffering, great or small. As we shall point out in the following message, the sufferings in which we share are for the building up of the Body of Christ. They are in no way related to the accomplishment of redemption.

II. THE STEWARD BEING A MINISTER

A. Of the Church

Speaking of the Body of Christ, the church, Paul says in 1:25, "Of which I became a minister according to the stewardship of God, which was given to me for you, to complete the word of God." Here Paul says that, as a steward, he became a minister of the church.

B. To Complete the Word of God

In 1:25 Paul also speaks of completing the word of God. The word of God is the divine revelation, which was not completed until the New Testament was written. In the New Testament the apostles, especially the Apostle Paul, completed the word of God in the mystery of God, which is Christ, and in the mystery of Christ, which is the church, to give us a full revelation of God's economy. According to 1:26, the word of God is the "mystery which has been hidden from the ages and from the generations, but now has been manifested to His saints." This hidden mystery is related to Christ and the church, the Head and the Body. The unveiling of this mystery through the Apostle Paul is a major part of the completion of the word of God as the divine revelation.

"From the ages" means from eternity, and "from the generations" means from the times. The mystery concerning Christ and the church was hidden from eternity and from all the times until the New Testament age, when it is being manifested to the saints, including all of us, the believers in Christ.

Prior to the time of Paul, the divine revelation had not been completed. Before Paul came forth to minister, God's revelation had already been given in the Old Testament. Furthermore, God had revealed Himself through the events recorded in the Gospels and in part of the Acts. However, it was necessary for Paul to write a number of Epistles concerning Christ as the mystery of God and concerning the church as the mystery of Christ in order for the divine revelation to be complete. This completion of the divine revelation is seen especially in four of his Epistles: Galatians, Ephesians, Philippians, and Colossians.

Although the divine revelation was completed through the apostles, especially through Paul, in a practical sense it also needs to be completed through us today. This means that as we contact people, we must progressively, continually, and gradually preach the word in full. To preach the word in full, or to fully preach the word, is to complete the word. Among so many Christians today there is surely a great need for such a completing of the word. Recently, a magazine stated that in the United States there are fifty million regenerated Christians. How many of them know God's purpose in saving them? Very few. In Christianity the word of God has been preached, but it has not been preached in full. The preaching of today's Christianity has not completed the word of God. Hence, there is an urgent need for this completion.

We have pointed out that the word of God which needs completion is the mystery spoken of in 1:26. Many Christians preach the word of God, but very few tell people what God's mystery is. The word of God preached in the full gospel is not related to escaping hell and going to heaven;

neither is it related to peace, joy, and a happy life. The word that needs to be completed is "the mystery which has been hidden from the ages and from the generations." This mystery is concealed, hidden. If it were not hidden, it would no longer be a mystery. The mystery concealed from ages and generations is the word of God that must now be completed through the preaching of the saints. This concealed mystery, which has been made manifest to God's saints, is "Christ in you, the hope of glory" (v. 27). Although I have heard the preaching of the gospel for years, I have rarely heard a message saying that when someone believes in Jesus Christ, Christ will not only save him, but also come into his spirit and remain there as his life. Most of the preaching in today's Christianity is not like this. Thus, there is the need for the completion of the word of God.

If we do not minister the riches of Christ to others, their knowledge of the divine revelation will be lacking. As far as the revelation itself is concerned, there is no lack. Everything was completed centuries ago. However, in practice, there may still be a lack, especially if we do not fulfill our part of the stewardship of God. We all need to fulfill our responsibility to complete the word of God.

The new ones in the Lord's recovery need the completion of the word of God. For example, a new one may firmly believe that Christ is God and the Creator. However, he may not realize the all-inclusiveness of Christ and experience Him as such an all-inclusive One. He may not realize that, as a man, Christ is also a creature. When he hears about this aspect of Christ, he may be troubled. This indicates that someone needs to complete the word of God to him in this matter and point out that, although Christ is God, He is still a man. He is all-inclusive. In 1 Timothy 2:5 Paul speaks of the man Christ Jesus. Furthermore, after the ascension of Christ, Stephen saw the Son of Man in the heavens (Acts 7:56). Surely a man is a creature with flesh and bones. After His resurrection, the Lord showed His disciples that He had a body of flesh and bones (Luke 24:39). Since the resurrected Christ is still a man with such a body, it is correct to say that He is a creature. Nevertheless, due to the influence of religious tradition, many believers may be reluctant to make such a statement about Christ. To them, such a teaching may be heretical. We need to help them take the pure Word of God and believe whatever it says. This means that we need to help them have the completion of the word of God.

In the Lord's recovery we need more stewards who are able to complete the word of God. We all must bear the burden for this. We need to spend more time in the Lord's presence so that He may become our portion for our enjoyment and so that we may have the riches of Christ to minister to others. In this way we shall become those who complete the word of God. Then through our ministry other believers will be nourished, strengthened, confirmed, and built up.

The Body is built up as all the members carry out the stewardship of ministering the riches of Christ. May there be such a mutual stewardship among us. You minister the riches of Christ to others, and they minister Christ to you. If this is our situation, we all shall be nourished and enjoy Christ more than ever. Then through the stewardship of dispensing the riches of Christ, the church will be built up in a practical way.

LIFE-STUDY OF COLOSSIANS

MESSAGE TWELVE

FILLING UP WHAT IS LACKING OF THE AFFLICTIONS OF CHRIST

Scripture Reading: Col. 1:24; 1 Pet. 3:18; Heb. 9:26; Isa. 53:3-5, 7-8; John 12:24; Luke 12:50; Phil. 3:10; Rev. 1:9; 2 Tim. 2:10; 2 Cor. 1:5-6

In 1:24 Paul says, "Now I rejoice in my sufferings on your behalf, and fill up that which is lacking of the afflictions of Christ in my flesh for His Body, which is the church." When I first read this verse, I was surprised and troubled. I wondered how there could be any lack in the sufferings of Christ. At the time, I was fully under the religious concept that it was impossible for Christ to have any lack. Nevertheless, in this verse Paul says clearly that he was to "fill up that which is lacking of the afflictions of Christ."

TWO KINDS OF SUFFERING

Are not the sufferings of Christ already complete? How can it be necessary for the afflictions of Christ on behalf of the Body to be completed? The Lord Jesus underwent two kinds of suffering: the suffering for redemption and the suffering for producing and building up the Body, the church. None of us can have any share in His suffering for redemption. To say that we can participate in this suffering is to speak blasphemy. He alone is the Redeemer, and the suffering for redemption was fully accomplished by Him. We are neither qualified nor positioned to share in the Lord's suffering for redemption. In typology, on the day of atonement, only the high priest, who made atonement for the people, was allowed to enter into the Holy of Holies. The high priest was a figure of Christ as the unique One capable of accomplishing redemption and qualified to do it.

A number of verses speak of Christ's sufferings for the accomplishment of redemption. For example, 1 Peter 3:18 says, "For Christ also hath once suffered for sins, the just for the unjust, that he might bring us to God." Christ, the righteous One, died for the unrighteous ones. He was the only One qualified to bear this kind of affliction. Hebrews 9:26 and Isaiah 53:3-5, 7-8 also indicate that Christ suffered to accomplish redemption on our behalf. In this suffering we have no share. It was borne by Christ alone.

Although we cannot participate in Christ's suffering for redemption, if we are faithful to Him, we must share in His suffering for the producing and building up of His Body. Paul was a pattern for us in this matter. Immediately after his conversion, he began to share in this suffering of Christ, to partake of the afflictions of Christ for the sake of His Body.

This is contrary to the concept that nothing related to Christ can be lacking. According to this concept, whatever Christ is and does is complete. But here is a word telling us that at least one thing related to Christ is lacking—His afflictions for producing and building up His Body. For the producing of His Body, Christ suffered a great deal. But because this suffering has not been completed by Christ Himself, there is the need for His faithful ones to make up this shortage. Paul did not suffer for redemption, but he did suffer for the producing and building up of the Body of Christ.

The Apostle Paul was a pattern for the believers to follow (1 Tim. 1:16). We must consider Paul as a pattern, not as someone who was so high that no one else can be like he was. Because by the Lord's mercy Paul was set up to be a pattern for us, whatever he was, we can be also. We must believe in the Lord's mercy. If the mercy of the Lord made Paul a pattern, then His mercy can accomplish in us the same thing that it did in Paul. This means that just as Paul suffered for the producing and building up of the Body of Christ, so we must also suffer for the church.

Christ, of course, took the lead to suffer for the producing and building up of His Body. But the apostles and believers must follow Christ's footsteps in suffering this kind of affliction. In John 12:24 the Lord Jesus said, "Truly, truly, I say to you, unless a grain of wheat falls into the ground and dies, it abides alone; but if it dies, it bears much fruit." This verse does not speak of Christ's redeeming death, but of His producing, generating death. Christ fell into the ground and died as a grain of wheat in order to produce many grains for the church. According to John 12:26, those who desire to serve Him must follow Him in this regard.

In Luke 12:50 the Lord Jesus said, "But I have a baptism to be baptized with; and how am I straightened till it be accomplished!" The word baptism in this verse refers to Christ's all-inclusive death on the cross, a death that was not only for redemption, but also for producing the Body through the release of the divine life. As the Lord's word to His disciples in Mark 10:38 and 39 makes clear, they also were to share in the baptism with which He Himself was to be baptized.

In Philippians 3:10 Paul speaks of knowing the fellowship of Christ's sufferings. These sufferings are not for redemption, but for the building up of the Body. We cannot have fellowship in Christ's sufferings for redemption, but we need to have much fellowship in Christ's sufferings for the church.

A JOINT PARTAKER OF TRIBULATION IN JESUS

In Revelation 1:9 John says that he was a "joint partaker in the tribulation and kingdom and endurance in Jesus." To say that we are joint partakers in the tribulation, kingdom, and endurance in Jesus indicates that we are suffering. When Jesus lived on earth as a man, He suffered continually. According to the history of His life, His name Jesus denotes a suffering person, a man of sorrows (Isa. 53:3). Therefore, to be a joint partaker of tribulation in Jesus is to suffer and to be persecuted as we follow Jesus the Nazarene. The book of Revelation is for those who are suffering tribulation in Jesus. As we wait for the coming of the Lord, we must be willing to suffer. This suffering is for the Body, the church. We must participate in the sufferings of Jesus for the sake of the church.

When Jesus was on earth, He was persecuted by the Jewish religion, a religion formed according to God's oracles. John 5:16 says that the Jews persecuted Jesus because He broke their Sabbath. Religious people cannot tolerate the breaking of their regulations. Any violation of their religious regulations will stir up persecution. When Jesus broke the Sabbath, the Jewish religionists persecuted Him and even sought to kill Him. Eventually, religion succeeded in sentencing Jesus to death.

Just as religion persecuted Jesus, it also persecutes the followers of Jesus. We know from the book of Acts that the Jews in the synagogues stood up in opposition to the apostles. Paul suffered this kind of persecution very much. John, the writer of Revelation, also experienced it. John was exiled to the island of Patmos "for the word of God and the testimony of Jesus." He became a joint partaker in the suffering, the affliction, in Jesus.

The persecution against the Lord Jesus originated not with the secular world, but with the religious world. In the book of Acts we see that the situation was the same regarding the persecution of the apostles. The opposition did not come mainly from the Gentiles, but from the Jewish religion. In like manner, a great many martyrs have suffered persecution at the hand of religion. Religion always persecutes the genuine followers of Jesus. Now it is our turn to undergo this persecution, this suffering for the building up of the Body of Christ. During the years I was with Brother Nee in China, I saw how much he was persecuted by religion. The rumors, opposition, and condemnation came from the religious people. In his subtlety, Satan, the Devil, uses religion to oppose and to persecute those who follow the Lord Jesus. Therefore, like John on the island of Patmos, we also must be joint partakers in the tribulation in Jesus. In this way we make up what is lacking of the afflictions of Christ for the church.

SUFFERING FOR THE SAINTS

In 2 Timothy 2:10 Paul says, "Therefore I endure all things for the elect's sake." This verse is a further indication that Paul suffered for the sake of the elect, God's chosen people.

Furthermore, 2 Corinthians 1:5 and 6 say, "For as the sufferings of Christ abound in us, so our consolation also aboundeth by Christ. And whether we be afflicted, it is for your consolation and salvation, which is effectual in the enduring of the same sufferings which we also suffer: or whether we be comforted, it is for your consolation and salvation." This is another indication of how much Paul suffered for the saints.

THE GOAL OF OUR WORK

We need to follow the early apostles in making up the lack of Christ's afflictions for the church. We also need to share in the fellowship of Christ's sufferings for the building up of the church. The goal of our Christian work must be the building up of the church. However, if we care only for such activities as preaching the gospel or teaching the Bible, we may be welcomed and appreciated. But if the goal of our preaching and teaching is the building up of the church, we shall be opposed by the religious ones.

What is our goal in preaching the gospel? It is not simply to save sinners from hell. It is to obtain material for the building up of the Body of Christ. When I was in religion, I heard many messages encouraging us to preach the gospel. We were always asked to consider God's love and sympathy for pitiful sinners, and we were told to have the same feeling toward them. Sometimes preachers would say, "Thousands are going to hell every day. Is your heart untouched by this?" Some would be inspired by this preaching and with tears respond to the altar call to become ministers of the gospel. The term "soul winning" is very common in today's Christianity. But what is the purpose of soul winning? Have you ever heard that soul winning is for Body building? Nevertheless, Paul's goal in preaching the gospel was the building up of the Body. This is why he was persecuted and why he suffered.

Surely the Jews were the people of God during the time of the Lord Jesus on earth. Did they not daily offer up sacrifices to God? Did they not have the temple which was built according to God's revelation and instruction? The answer to these questions is yes. But one day Jesus came. He did not care for the temple in the way the Jewish religionists did. When His disciples were admiring the buildings of the temple, He said, "A stone shall by no means be left upon a stone which shall not be thrown down" (Matt. 24:2). Who could have dared to say this? If you had been there and had spoken these words, the Jews would have killed you. This was the reason they persecuted the Lord Jesus.

In the book of Acts we see that those in the Jewish synagogues accused the Apostle Paul of being a "pestilent fellow" (Acts 24:5). Wherever Paul went, he caused trouble. Therefore, he was opposed by the religious people, by the so-called people of God.

It is the same today. If we preach the gospel only for the sake of soul winning and rescuing people from hell, we probably shall not suffer very much. In fact, we may find ourselves welcomed in many places. However, if we take the building of the Body as the goal of gospel preaching, we must be prepared to suffer, even to be opposed and persecuted. Religion does not agree with the building up of the Body. Some Christians have even lied about us, classifying us with those in cults and evil, blasphemous movements. In 2 Corinthians 6:8 Paul said that he had experienced both evil report and good report. If, as you serve the Lord, others give only good reports concerning you, I would question your faithfulness to the Lord. If you are faithful to the Lord, today's religion will criticize you and spread evil reports about you.

Apparently, religion is for God; actually, it is against God's economy. Nothing is more subtle and damaging to God's economy than religion. Winning souls does not affect religion; rather, it helps it a great deal. But whenever you talk about the building up of the Body, religion is threatened.

Consider what Paul did when he was Saul of Tarsus. He was a leader in his religion, and he did everything possible to derive benefit from that religion. However, on the way to Damascus, he was caught by the Lord. After his conversion, whatever he did amounted to a tearing down of religion. Paul was bold. The Lord Jesus annulled the Sabbath day, but Paul annulled something even more important to Judaism—Paul annulled circumcision. The Jews condemned Paul for teaching others to discontinue the practice of circumcision. If Paul had been concerned only with soul winning, he would not have offended people. Paul did not say, "I must keep all the doors open. Therefore, I shouldn't say a word about circumcision. I must not say anything contrary to the Jewish religion. For the sake of soul winning, I must maintain a good relationship with the religious people." If Paul's concern was merely the saving of souls, this could have been his practice. But since he was for the building up of the Body, there was no way for him to do this. For the sake of the producing and building up of the Body of Christ, Paul shared in the sufferings of Christ.

Often people have told me that they appreciated my ministry with the exception of my ministry concerning the church. Some have even pleaded with me not to speak of the church. One instance of this took place in Texas in 1964. I had been invited to Dallas to speak to a certain group of Christians. One evening after the meeting, my host said to me, "Brother Lee, we appreciate your ministry. However, we wish to make it clear that this audience cannot accept any word about the church. In your messages, please don't say anything about the church." I replied, "It is important for you to realize that the more I minister on Christ as life, the more the saints will hunger for the church." During the last meeting, I had the Lord's leading to speak on the Body from Romans 12. I knew that if I did not speak regarding the church, I would not be faithful to the Lord or honest to the audience. Although I knew my host and others would be offended, I proceeded to speak a strong word about the church life. Unhappy with my speaking, my host did not even rise up to see us off when we departed early the next morning. Nevertheless, one brother was greatly helped by that message on the church and, as a result, was encouraged to turn to the way of the Lord's recovery.

For the sake of the Body of Christ, the church, we need to fill up what is lacking of the afflictions of Christ. I can testify that I have been attacked and opposed simply because of my stand for the recovery of the church life. If you choose to stand for the church, be prepared for attack, misunderstanding, and rumors. Many evil things will be spoken concerning you. The reason for this is that the matter of the church stirs up the authority of darkness. Therefore, those who stand for the church must be prepared for the attack of the enemy. The Lord Jesus said, "On this rock I will build My church, and the gates of Hades shall not prevail against it" (Matt. 16:18). This word indicates that the gates of Hades, the power of darkness, will do everything possible to frustrate the building up of the church. Praise the Lord that He has promised that the gates of Hades will not prevail!

If we are faithful and honest with respect to the Lord's ministry and the stewardship of God for the building up of the church, we shall suffer attack, opposition, and evil speaking. In view of this, we need to look to the Lord that we may be covered by His prevailing blood. We also need to pray that the Lord may hide us in Himself as our high tower. As we hide in the Lord during times of suffering and affliction, we share in the fellowship of His sufferings. In this way we fill up what is lacking of the afflictions of Christ for the sake of the church.

LIFE-STUDY OF COLOSSIANS

MESSAGE THIRTEEN

COMPLETING THE WORD OF GOD

Scripture Reading: Col. 1:25; 1 Cor. 15:45b; 2 Cor. 3:17; 13:14; Eph. 3:14-19

In 1:25 Paul says, "Of which I became a minister according to the stewardship of God, which was given to me for you, to complete the word of God." In this message we shall consider the matter of completing the word of God.

I. THE WORD OF GOD INCLUDING THE OLD TESTAMENT AND THE WORD PREACHED BY THE EARLY DISCIPLES

At the time of Paul, the word of God included the Old Testament and the word preached by the early disciples. In Acts 4:29 the disciples prayed that they might preach God's word with boldness. According to Acts 4:31, "they were all filled with the Holy Spirit, and they spake the word of God with boldness." In Acts 6:4 we see that the apostles gave themselves to prayer and to the ministry of the word. Acts 6:7 tells us that "the word of God increased." Those who were scattered because of the persecution against the church following the death of Stephen "went every where preaching the word" (Acts 8:4). Furthermore, Acts 12:24 says that "the word of God grew and multiplied."

Although the word of God preached by the early disciples grew and multiplied, it was not yet completed according to God's economy. For this completion, God's revelation to Paul was needed. Because the Jews have only the Old Testament, they do not have the complete oracle of God. Moreover, although Christians have both the Old Testament and the New Testament, in actuality many of them do not have the complete revelation of God. In their experience and in their understanding, they may have only the Gospels, Acts, and part of Romans. Many have studied the Bible, but still lack an adequate understanding of the divine revelation.

According to the stewardship of God, Paul became a minister of the church to complete the word of God. Consider what a lack there would be if we did not have the Epistles of Paul. Without them, there would be no completion of the word of God. Paul's stewardship was to complete the word of God in order to dispense Christ with all His riches into the churches. The revelation given to Paul was for the completion of God's word. Therefore, it is crucial that we all know the revelation that was given to Paul.

II. GOD'S REVELATION TO PAUL

A. Christ Being the Mystery of God

Paul received the revelation of Christ as the mystery of God. In 2:2 he speaks of the "full knowledge of the mystery of God, Christ." This term, the mystery of God, is not found in the Old Testament. The Gospels do not record any time that it was used by the Lord Jesus. It was first used by Paul in his Epistles. The mystery of God is Christ as the embodiment of God. Colossians 2:9 says, "For in Him dwells all the fullness of the Godhead bodily."

As the mystery of God, Christ must be both the embodiment of God and the life-giving Spirit (1 Cor. 15:45b; 2 Cor. 3:17). All fundamental Christian teachers believe that Christ is the embodiment of God, but very few see that He is also the life-giving Spirit. In order for us to know Christ in reality as the embodiment of God, we need to experience Him as the life-giving Spirit. Because the enemy knows the crucial significance of this, he attacks this point intensely. If we do not realize that Christ is the life-giving Spirit, the fact that Christ is the embodiment of God is merely doctrine or theory. It is just an objective teaching not at all related to our Christian experience. If this is the situation, there is no way for theory to become reality. The reality of Christ as the embodiment of God is in Christ as the life-giving Spirit.

In John 14:16 through 18 the Lord Jesus said, "And I will ask the Father, and He will give you another Comforter, that He may be with you forever; even the Spirit of reality, Whom the world cannot receive, because it does not behold Him or know Him; but you know Him, because He abides with you and shall be in you. I will not leave you orphans; I am coming to you." The One who is the Spirit of reality in verse 17 becomes the very One who is the Lord Himself in verse 18; He becomes I. This indicates that after His resurrection the Lord became the Spirit of reality. First Corinthians 15:45, which deals with the matter of resurrection, confirms this by saying that the last Adam became a life-giving Spirit. Paul was bold and not at all ambiguous in declaring the fact that Christ is the Spirit. To the natural mind it is not logical that the last Adam, a man in the flesh, could become a life-giving Spirit. Nevertheless, Paul uncompromisingly declared this fact. Furthermore, in 2 Corinthians 3:17 he said, "Now the Lord is that Spirit." According to the context of the whole chapter, the Spirit in verse 17 is the Spirit who gives life in verse 6. Furthermore, in 2 Timothy 4:22 Paul clearly said, "The Lord be with thy spirit." How clear is Paul's word!

In 1964 I was warned by an intimate friend not to teach that Christ is the Spirit. This one admitted that the Bible teaches that Christ is the Spirit. However, because religious tradition makes others unwilling to accept this fact, he was not bold to declare it. I told my friend, "If I do not teach that Christ is the life-giving Spirit, I have no ministry. I came to this country with the burden mainly to minister along this line." Later that year I gave a series of messages on Christ as the Spirit. These messages are printed in *The Economy of God.*

Many of us can testify of the help we have received in life through realizing that our Lord today is the life-giving Spirit in our spirit. If Christ were not the Spirit in our spirit, how could we experience Him as our life? We would have no experience of Christ as life. Instead, we would simply have another form of religious practice. But because we have Christ as the life-giving Spirit, we do not have a religion. We have the living Christ in our experience. On the one hand, He is the embodiment of the fullness of God and, on the other hand, He is the life-giving Spirit indwelling our spirit. This revelation of Christ is part of the revelation given to Paul for the completion of the word of God.

B. The Dispensation of God

Paul was also given the revelation concerning the dispensation of God (2 Cor. 13:14; Eph. 3:14-19). The word dispensation has been damaged through misuse. To many Christians it refers simply to the ways in which God deals with people, ways that are called dispensations. When we use the word dispensation, however, we use it with the meaning of dispensing. In His economy, God is dispensing Himself into us. Paul was the first to speak of God's dispensation, and his writings reveal that God is now dispensing Himself into our being. For example, 2 Corinthians 13:14 says, "The grace of the Lord Jesus Christ, and the love of God, and the fellowship of the Holy Spirit, be with you all" (Gk.). This is the dispensing of the Triune God into our being. Where else in the Bible can you find such a clear word concerning the dispensation of the Triune God into the believers? In this verse we have the Father as the source, the Son as the course, and the Spirit as the flow. What a dispensation!

In Ephesians 3:14-19 Paul also speaks of God's dispensation. He prays to the Father that we may be strengthened with power by His Spirit into our inner man so that Christ may make His home in our hearts. The result is that we are rooted and grounded in love and are strong to apprehend with all the saints what is the breadth, length, height, and depth, and to know the knowledge-surpassing love of Christ so that we may be filled unto all the fullness of God. In these verses Paul speaks of the Triune God—the Father, the Spirit, and Christ (the Son). Through the dispensation of the Triune God into our being, we become the fullness of God, His expression.

C. The Church Being the Mystery of Christ

In Ephesians 3:4 Paul speaks of the mystery of Christ. The mystery of God in Colossians 2:2 is Christ, whereas the mystery of Christ in Ephesians 3:4 is the church. In Ephesians 1:22 and 23 Paul says that the church is the Body of Christ, His fullness. Paul was the first to use such a term to describe the church. Nowhere in the writings of Peter or John are we told that the church is the Body. Although Paul came on the scene later than the original apostles, he was bold to speak forth the divine revelation and dared to use terminology that had not been used before. Recognizing this, Peter recommended Paul, saying in his second Epistle, "Even as our beloved brother Paul also according to the wisdom given unto him hath written unto you; as also in all his epistles, speaking in them of these things; in which are some things hard to be understood" (2 Pet. 3:15-16). Peter could write these words even though he had once been rebuked by Paul (Gal. 2:11). Because Paul was not afraid to utter the revelation God had given him regarding the church, he was the kind of person the Lord could use to complete His word.

Another revolutionary term used by Paul concerning the church is the new man (Col. 3:10). Paul received the revelation that the church is the new man with Christ as the constituent. Only Paul had the boldness to use such a term.

There is an urgent need today for the completion of the word of God. Although Paul was used in the completion of the divine revelation centuries ago, there is still the need for its completion in a practical way among Christians today. In most Christian groups there is very little ministry of Christ as life. Furthermore, not many dare to face the issue of the church. Through his subtlety, Satan, the enemy of God, is seeking to nullify the completion of the word of God. The enemy may allow Christians to preach what is revealed in the Old Testament, in the Gospels, and in the Acts. But he cannot tolerate the teaching concerning Christ as the all-inclusive life-giving Spirit or concerning the church as the mystery of Christ.

Anyone who ministers along this line will be attacked by the enemy.

Because of my stand for the church, I have been the target of many evil rumors. I have been accused of twisting Brother Nee's teaching about the church life. Some claim that after World War II Brother Nee changed his concept regarding the ground of the church. According to this rumor, because I have not changed my attitude about the church ground, I have become different from Brother Nee in this matter. As an exposure of this false report, we put out *Further Talks on the Church Life,* which includes a number of messages on the church given by Brother Nee after World War II. Each of these messages is documented with the date and the place. After this book was released, the opposers changed their strategy and began to say that this book is not an accurate translation, but my own interpretation. However, those familiar with both English and Chinese can testify that the translation is very accurate and true to the original. These rumors show that Satan attacks those today who stand for the revelation given by God to Paul, in particular for the revelation concerning Christ as the mystery of God and the church as the mystery of Christ.

Many oppose us because they have been drugged by religious tradition. Under the influence of this tradition, they condemn as heretical the teaching that corresponds to the word completed by the Apostle Paul. Many of us can testify that in Christianity we did not receive the complete revelation, the completed word of God. It is the subtlety of the enemy to veil the word which was completed through Paul. For this reason, we are burdened for the completion of the word of God.

In 1:29 Paul said that he labored, "struggling according to His operation which operates in me in power." Paul labored and struggled for the completion of the word of God. The Greek word indicates that he was wrestling, engaging in combat, for this completion. We can frankly testify that we also are wrestling for the completion of the revelation given to Paul. Apparently in the Lord's ministry we are working;

actually we are fighting against religion with its tradition. We need to be clear, however, that our wrestling is not against blood and flesh, but against the evil powers in the heavenlies, against the gates of Hades that seek to destroy the church. As we struggle and fight, our burden, our stewardship, is to complete the word of God. What we are ministering today is the completion of the divine revelation given to Paul.

We need to point out again and again that this revelation concerns Christ as the embodiment of God and the church as the expression of Christ. Although there are a great many Christian activities in this country, there is hardly any completing of the word of God. Who is bearing the burden to declare that Christ the Savior is the life-giving Spirit imparting the divine life into us? Who is discharging the burden to tell the Lord's people that they should be the living Body to express Christ on the proper ground in each locality? We in the Lord's recovery must take up the responsibility for this. The goal of the Lord's recovery is the completion of the word of God. I hope that many brothers will rise up to fulfill this ministry.

Today there is much gospel preaching, Bible teaching, and Christian work, but where is the completion of the word of God? There are thousands of so-called churches, but there is no completion of God's word. Without the completion of the word of God, God's purpose cannot be fulfilled, and Christ cannot obtain His Bride or come with His kingdom. We need to experience Christ as the all-inclusive, life-giving Spirit and stand with the church on the proper ground. No matter how much we are opposed and attacked, we must stand with the church and experience Christ in our daily life.

III. THE COMPLETION OF THE WORD OF GOD

The completion of the word of God includes the great mystery of Christ and the church (Eph. 5:32); the full revelation concerning Christ, the Head (Col. 1:26-27; 2:19; 3:11); and the full revelation concerning the church, the Body

(Eph. 3:3-6). Not only should these matters be impressed upon us; they should be infused into our being. May the Lord make us all clear concerning His recovery and concerning the wrestling for the completion of the word of God. If we would be those who complete the word of God, we must minister Christ as the life-giving Spirit and stand with the church as the living expression of Christ on the proper ground of locality. This is our burden, our ministry, and our warfare.

LIFE-STUDY OF COLOSSIANS

MESSAGE FOURTEEN

CHRIST—THE MYSTERY OF GOD'S ECONOMY

Scripture Reading: Col. 1:25-29

In this message we come to the mystery of God's economy, the mystery that is actually Christ Himself.

In 1:25 Paul speaks of the stewardship of God. The Greek word rendered stewardship, *oikonomia,* may also be rendered economy or administration. The stewardship is the economy, and God's economy is His dispensation. God's intention in His economy is to dispense Himself—the Father, the Son, and the Spirit—into His chosen people.

Christ is the mystery, the secret, and the crucial focus, of the divine economy. This means that the secret of the dispensation of the Triune God into God's chosen people is Christ Himself. Christ is the focal point of God's dispensation. God's dispensation is altogether related to Christ and focused on Him.

For centuries, Christians have been reading the Epistles of Paul, but very few have seen the matter of God's economy and Christ as the mystery of this economy. I can testify that I read Ephesians and Colossians for years before I began to see that Christ is the mystery of God's economy. Early in my Christian life, I did not see that Christ is the secret of God's dispensation. This matter is hidden and is not according to our natural concept. In order to see it we need to pray and to exercise our spirit as we study the Epistle of Colossians in a detailed way. Let us now consider 1:25-29 in some detail.

A MINISTER OF THE CHURCH

Verse 25 says, "Of which I became a minister according to the stewardship of God, which was given to me for you, to complete the word of God." The word "which" refers to the church in verse 24. This indicates that Paul became a minister, not of a certain mission work or of a particular work of teaching and preaching, but of the church. The word minister describes one who serves. Paul became such a minister of the church according to the stewardship, the economy, the dispensation, of God. This stewardship was given to Paul for the church. The goal of God's stewardship for the church was to complete the word of God.

THE MYSTERY MANIFESTED TO THE SAINTS

Notice that verse 25 does not end with a period, but with a comma. Then in verse 26 Paul continues, "The mystery which has been hidden from the ages and from the generations, but now has been manifested to His saints." According to grammar, the mystery in verse 26 is in apposition to the word of God in verse 25. This means that the word of God is the very mystery which has been hidden from the ages and generations, but is now made manifest to the saints. The ages here denote eternity, whereas the generations denote the times. The mystery concerning Christ and the church had been hidden from eternity and from all times until the New Testament age, when it was manifested to the saints, the believers in Christ.

It is important that in verse 26 Paul does not say that the mystery has been manifested to the apostles; he says that it has been manifested to the saints. Due to the influence of religious tradition, many believe that such things as God's economy cannot be understood by the so-called laymen. How we thank the Lord that the mystery has been manifested to the saints, to all those who believe in Christ! Even the youngest ones among us have both the position to see this mystery and the privilege of seeing it. We have the privilege of seeing something that was not revealed to Adam, Noah, Abraham, Moses, or to the prophets such as Isaiah, Jeremiah, and Zechariah. Praise the Lord that we can know the completion of the word of God! We can know Christ as the mystery of God's economy and the Body as Christ's fullness. Furthermore, we can know that the church is the new man with Christ as the content and constituent. None of these things was made known to God's people in the Old Testament age.

Today we focus our attention upon Christ as the mystery of God and upon the church as the mystery of Christ. As the mystery of God, the all-inclusive Christ is the embodiment of God and also the life-giving Spirit. As the mystery of Christ, the church is the Body of Christ, His fullness, and the new man to be the full expression of Christ as well. This is the mystery that has been made manifest to the saints.

Paul's writing in this Epistle is quite complex. He uses many long sentences with various clauses and relative pronouns. Actually, verses 24 through 29 should be regarded as a single sentence. In verse 27, the continuation of verse 26, Paul says, "To whom God willed to make known what are the riches of the glory of this mystery among the nations, which is Christ in you, the hope of glory." The word "whom" at the beginning of this verse refers to the saints mentioned in the preceding verse. To us God has willed to make known the riches of the glory of this mystery. This mystery, which is Christ in us as the hope of glory, is made known among the nations. The word "which" in verse 27 refers to the mystery. This mystery full of glory among the nations is Christ in us. Christ in us is mysterious and glorious as well. Because Paul was dealing with matters deep and profound, his writing was complex, and his sentences were long.

THE RICHES OF THE GLORY OF THE MYSTERY

Let us now pay closer attention to the riches of the glory of the mystery spoken of in verse 27. The riches of this mystery among the nations are the riches of all that Christ is to the Gentile believers (Eph. 3:8). At the time Paul wrote to the Colossians, the Jews regarded the Gentiles, the nations, as swine. Nevertheless, Paul says that God has willed to make known the riches of the glory of this mystery among the nations, that is, among the Gentile "swine." Various terms could be used to describe the Gentiles: sinners, rebels, enemies of God, sons of disobedience, sons of wrath. Before we were saved, we were in this category. But even among such people

God has willed to make known the riches of the glory of this mystery.

After you were saved, did you not have the sense that you had entered into glory? Many of us had this kind of experience. Although we were sinners, enemies, and rebels, we have become sons of God. We are also heirs of God, joint partakers of Christ, and even the members of Christ. Furthermore, the New Testament reveals that we are priests and kings. As heirs of God, we shall inherit not only God Himself, but all things. We are sons of God, heirs of God, partners of Christ, and priests and kings. What a glory this is!

If we see this glory, we shall also know the riches of the glory, even though we lack the language to utter these riches adequately. These riches include the divine life, the divine nature, the anointing, and the all-inclusive Spirit. Other aspects of the riches are righteousness, justification, holiness, sanctification, transformation, glorification, comfort, and the divine Presence. It is impossible to list all the riches. They are beyond counting. These are the riches of the unique glory, the glory that is ours because we are sons and heirs of God, partners of Christ, and priests and kings.

The key to the riches of glory is Christ Himself. Although the Jews in ancient times were the people of God and not Gentile "swine," they did not recognize the Lord Jesus as their Messiah. To many Jews today, the term Messiah has no reality. When their Messiah comes and they recognize Him, He will only be among them. But 1:27 indicates that Christ is not merely among us; He is in us. To us Christ is not only the objective One, but also the subjective One dwelling in us. We need to tell the Jews that instead of waiting for their Messiah to come only in an outward way, they too can have Christ, the true Messiah, dwelling in them right now and thereby become sons of God. The Jews who receive Christ into them will not only be the people of God chosen by Him, but also the sons of God regenerated by Him. What a glory it is to be indwelt by Christ!

As believers in Christ, we know the riches of the glory of this mystery. We cannot exhaust the items of the riches of such a glory. All the blessings in the Bible are included in the riches of this glory, which is our portion. This glory is the glory of the mystery among the nations, and this mystery is Christ in us. The Christ who dwells within us is the mystery full of glory, with countless riches. This is the key point in the book of Colossians.

BACK TO THE MYSTERY

Those in Colosse, however, had lost the vision of this mystery and had become distracted by philosophy, observances, ordinances, and practices. They had been defrauded and carried away as spoil from their prize, the enjoyment of the all-inclusive Christ. Like the Colossians, today's Christians have also lost the vision of the glory of Christ as the mystery of God's economy. The vast majority of genuine Christians have been distracted and carried away to things other than Christ Himself. Because the Colossians had been distracted, Paul wrote to say that the mystery hidden from the ages and from the generations has been made manifest to the saints. This mystery is the all-inclusive Christ who indwells us. Because we have the One who is all in all, we have no need to turn to philosophies, ordinances, observances, and practices. How I look to the Lord that we all may be brought back to this mystery! Let us forget everything other than Christ and care only for Him. Christ, the mystery among the Gentiles, has a glory filled with riches.

THE HOPE OF GLORY

In verse 27 Paul says that Christ in us is the hope of glory. Christ is the mystery which is full of glory now. This glory will be manifested to its fullest extent when Christ returns to glorify His saints (Rom. 8:30). Hence, it is a hope, the hope of glory. Christ Himself is also this hope of glory.

Today we may live in Christ, by Christ, and with Christ. We may live Him, grow Him, and produce Him. At the same time, He is our hope of glory. If we see the vision that the all-inclusive Christ who indwells us is our hope of glory, our living will be revolutionized. We shall say, "Lord, from now on I won't care for anything other than You. I won't care for doctrines, ordinances, regulations, or traditions. I don't care for religion, philosophy, or the elements of the world. Lord, I care only for You as the embodiment of God and as the life-giving Spirit in my spirit. Because You are so real, living, and practical in my spirit, I can live by You and with You. Lord, my only desire is to experience You in this way."

Eventually, the New Testament charges us to walk according to the mingled spirit (Gal. 5:16, 25; Rom. 8:4). We need to walk according to the Christ who is the very glory filled with riches. Oh, may we all see this vision! Once we have seen this vision, it will control every aspect of our daily walk.

If we see this vision, we shall also realize how much Christians today have been distracted to things other than Christ. They may pay their attention to good things, scriptural things, fundamental things, even spiritual things. Nevertheless, these things are not Christ Himself. It is crucial that we see the Christ who is the mystery hidden from eternity but now made manifest to the saints in the New Testament age. God has willed to make known among the nations the riches of the glory of this mystery, which is Christ in us as the hope of glory. This mystery is the key to our Christian life and also to the church life.

PRESENTING EVERY MAN FULL-GROWN IN CHRIST

In verse 28 Paul says that he announced Christ. Here Paul does not say that he taught Christ or preached Christ, but that he announced Christ. As he announced Him, he was "warning every man and teaching every man in all wisdom" in order to "present every man full-grown in Christ." Paul's ministry, whether in announcing Christ or in warning and teaching every man in all wisdom, was to minister Christ to others so that they could be perfect and complete by maturing with Christ unto full growth.

To become full-grown in Christ is a matter of life. Christ must be added into us. Then we need to grow in Christ and gradually gain more of the stature of Christ. Eventually, as Christ is wrought into us, we shall become full-grown in Christ.

The goal of Paul's ministry was to present every man full-grown in Christ. Whenever I consider this phrase, "present every man full-grown," as used in this verse, I sense how short I am. I am warned by the Spirit within me regarding my ministry. I am concerned about how many I shall be able to present full-grown in Christ. The burden of this responsibility weighs upon me greatly. Inwardly I am charged to announce Christ and to warn others and teach them regarding Christ so that I may present them full-grown in Christ.

Paul's concept in 1:28 is completely different from that held by Christian ministers and pastors today. Paul's concept concerning his ministry was that of dispensing Christ into others so that they may grow in Christ to maturity. He knew that Christ had to be added into the believers until they became full-grown in Christ. We need to have the same concept as Paul. As the elders care for the saints in the churches, they should seek to present all the dear ones full-grown in Christ.

STRUGGLING ACCORDING TO HIS OPERATION

In verse 29 Paul goes on to say, "For which also I labor, struggling according to His operation which operates in me in power." I believe that the words "for which" refer to the matter of presenting every man full-grown in Christ. For such a presentation Paul labored, struggled, fought, and wrestled. Paul's struggling, however, was according to Christ's operation within him. Hallelujah, the indwelling Christ is operating within us! This operating is His energizing. As He energizes us from within, we need to labor in cooperation with His operating.

The operation of Christ operates in power. The Greek word for power is the source of the English word dynamo. This power is no doubt the power of the resurrection life (Phil. 3:10), which operates within the apostle and all the believers (Eph. 1:19; 3:7, 20). By such an inward operating power of life Christ operates within us. This power is different from God's creating power. God's creating power is the source of the material things in our environment, whereas

God's resurrection power accomplishes the spiritual things for the church within our being. Paul labored, struggled, wrestled, and fought according to this resurrection power. By means of the operation in this power he carried out his ministry to present every saint full-grown in Christ.

May our eyes be opened to see that the goal of our work and ministry must be to minister Christ to others so that they may grow with the measure of Christ, who is the mystery of God's economy.

LIFE-STUDY OF COLOSSIANS

MESSAGE FIFTEEN

CHRIST IN YOU THE HOPE OF GLORY

Scripture Reading: Col. 1:26-27, 12, 15, 18-19; 2:2, 9, 16-17; 3:11; John 14:17, 20; 1 Cor. 15:45b; Phil. 1:19; 2 Tim. 4:22; 1 Cor. 6:17; Col. 3:4; Eph. 3:17a; Rom. 8:23; Phil. 3:21; 2 Thes. 1:10a

In the foregoing message we saw that Christ is the mystery of God's economy. In this message we shall go on to see that Christ in us is the hope of glory. In order to be impressed with this aspect of Christ, we need to pay attention to a number of crucial points regarding Christ that are covered in Colossians.

I. CHRIST, THE PORTION OF THE SAINTS

Christ is the portion of the saints. Colossians 1:12 says, "Giving thanks to the Father, Who qualified you for a share of the portion of the saints in the light." This is the first aspect of Christ presented in this Epistle. The word portion denotes Christ as the lot of the saints in the good land, flowing with milk and honey. The very Christ who indwells us is such a good land. He is the all-inclusive Christ for our enjoyment.

II. CHRIST, THE IMAGE OF THE INVISIBLE GOD

According to 1:15, Christ is also the image of the invisible God. This means that Christ is the expression of God. Although God is invisible, He is expressed in Christ. The very Christ who is our good land is also the image of the Triune God, His expression. As God's expression, Christ is the image of God.

III. CHRIST, THE FIRSTBORN OF ALL CREATION

Colossians 1:15 also says that Christ is the "firstborn of all creation." The invisible God is expressed in His creation. Romans 1:20 says, "For the invisible things of Him from the creation of the world, being apprehended by the things made, are clearly seen, both His eternal power and divine nature." God is expressed through His creation, and Christ is the firstborn of this creation. Thus, Christ is the means by which God expresses Himself. The fact that the image of God and the firstborn of creation are mentioned in the same verse indicates that the image of God is related to creation. This indicates clearly that as the firstborn of God's creation, Christ is the image of God, His expression.

IV. CHRIST, THE FIRSTBORN FROM AMONG THE DEAD

There are two creations of God: the old creation and the new creation. Unbelievers know only of the first creation, the creation of the universe. However, according to the Bible, God also has a new creation, which is the church. Christ is the firstborn not only of the old creation, but also of the new creation. As the firstborn of both creations, Christ is God's expression.

Verses 15 through 20 are closely connected and express one complete thought. In verses 15 and 16 we see that Christ is the image of the invisible God, the firstborn of all creation, because all things were created in Him. Notice that verses 17 and 18 each begin with the conjunction "and." Finally, in verse 19, Paul presents the conclusion of this line of thought: "For in Him all the fullness was pleased to dwell."

Paul's use of the word all in the phrase "all the fullness" indicates that the fullness both in the old creation and in the new creation dwells in Christ. We have pointed out that fullness is equal to image and also to expression. According to New Testament usage, the fullness also denotes the Body. In Ephesians 1:23 Paul says that the church is Christ's Body, "the fullness of the One Who fills all in all." The Body is the fullness, the fullness is the expression, and the expression is the image. If we would understand Colossians 1:15-20, we must see that the image in verse 15 denotes the very fullness as the expression in verse 19. Hence, the image of God is the expression of God, and this expression is the fullness of God. The fullness of God is seen in the old creation because Christ is the firstborn of creation and also in the new creation because Christ is the firstborn from among the dead. For this reason, verse 19 speaks of all the fullness. All the fullness was pleased to dwell in the all-inclusive Christ.

If we have the proper spiritual perspective, we shall see Christ when we look at the universe. Likewise, when we consider the church, we shall also see Christ. Both in the universe and in the church there is the fullness of God, His expression. This expression is the very Christ who is the image of the invisible God.

Every thoughtful person realizes that there is some kind of expression in the universe. The more we consider the universe, the more we are conscious that it is the expression of something. According to Colossians, the universe is the expression of the fullness of the invisible God. In the same principle, when we view the proper church life, we are also conscious of a certain expression. This expression is also that of the image of the invisible God. This image is Christ. Because Christ is the firstborn of both the old creation and the new creation, He is the expression of the invisible God.

V. CHRIST, IN WHOM ALL THE FULLNESS WAS PLEASED TO DWELL

Colossians 1:19 says that all the fullness was pleased to dwell in Christ. This thought is echoed in 2:9, where Paul says, "For in Him dwells all the fullness of the Godhead bodily." The fullness both in the old creation and in the new creation dwells in Christ. This fullness refers not to the riches of God, but to the expression of these riches. The expression of God's riches dwells in Christ.

Many Christians speak of the indwelling Christ without realizing that the Christ who indwells them is the all-inclusive One. If some were asked what kind of Christ lives in them, they would speak only of Christ as the Savior and the Redeemer. This, of course, is not wrong, but it is very inadequate. When Paul says, "Christ in you, the hope of glory" (1:27), he is referring to a very rich Christ, to the Christ who is our good land, the expression of the invisible God, the firstborn of both the old creation and the new creation, and the One in whom all the fullness is pleased to dwell. Even these items do not exhaust all that Christ is. It is the Christ with all these aspects who dwells in us to be our hope of glory.

VI. CHRIST, THE MYSTERY OF GOD'S ECONOMY

Many Christians, even Christian pastors and ministers, do not know what the mystery of God's economy is. Some are not even familiar with this term. The mystery of God's economy is Christ. The Christ who indwells us is the mystery of this economy, an economy that involves God's administration of the whole universe. How profound! God has a universal economy, and the center, the focal point, of this economy is Christ. Furthermore, this economy is abstract, profound, and mysterious. The mystery of this universal economy, its indescribable element, is Christ. The Colossians were very foolish in turning from such a Christ to Gnosticism, mysticism, and asceticism. What need did they have for philosophy when they had the very Christ who is the mystery of God's universal economy? How vital it is for us to realize that the very Christ who is the mystery of God's economy dwells in us!

VII. CHRIST, THE MYSTERY OF GOD

In 2:2 Paul speaks of the "full knowledge of the mystery of God, Christ." As the mystery of God, Christ is the embodiment of God and also the life-giving Spirit. Although we find it easy to speak of many things, it is difficult for us to speak of Christ as God's mystery. Concerning this, our mind is like a block of marble that is not able to absorb liquid. Although we may hear message after message about Christ as the mystery of God, we may not apprehend anything we hear.

Many years ago I met a certain brother who was fond of repeating the phrase, "Christ in me, the hope of glory." However, this brother had very little knowledge of Christ. Although he liked to talk about the indwelling Christ, he did not truly know Christ in this aspect. He did not realize that the Christ who lived in Him is the very mystery of God.

VIII. CHRIST, THE REALITY OF ALL POSITIVE THINGS

Colossians 2:16 and 17 say, "Let no one therefore judge you in eating and in drinking or in respect of a feast or of a new moon or of Sabbaths, which are a shadow of things to come, but the body is of Christ." These verses indicate that Christ is the reality of all positive things. He is the real sun, air, water, food, flowers, and trees. Compared to Christ, all the different trees are shadows. He is the real apple tree, fig tree, olive tree, pomegranate tree, and vine tree. In fact, He is the tree of life. He is also the reality of all the positive people in the Old Testament. For example, He is both the greater Solomon and the greater Jonah (Matt. 12:41-42).

In this Epistle, Paul was telling the Colossians that they were misguided in turning away from such an all-inclusive Christ to philosophy, observances, and the worship of angels. Why should they be subject to regulations about eating, drinking, feasts, new moons, and Sabbaths when all such things are shadows of spiritual things in Christ? There was no need for the Colossians to go back to those things because they had Christ, and Christ is everything.

IX. CHRIST, THE CONSTITUENT OF THE NEW MAN

In 3:10 and 11 Paul speaks of the new man, "where there cannot be Greek and Jew, circumcision and uncircumcision, barbarian, Scythian, slave, freeman, but Christ is all and in all." This indicates that Christ is the constituent of the new man. The new man is constituted with Christ as his essence and his very element. There was no need for the Colossians to be occupied with natural or cultural differences among the various peoples. In the new man there is room only for Christ. Because Christ is all and in all in the new man, there is no room for the natural man in any way. Christ is every member, and He is in every member. The Christ who indwells us is such a constituent of the new man.

X. CHRIST IN YOU

What a Christ we have within us! The Christ who indwells us has all the aspects covered in this message. He is the portion of the saints, the image of the invisible God, the firstborn of all creation, the firstborn from among the dead, the One in whom God's fullness dwells, the mystery of God's economy, the mystery of God, the reality of all positive things, and the constituent of the new man. Although all these aspects of Christ are revealed in the book of Colossians, we did not see most of them because they are not according to our natural concept. What corresponds to our concept is Paul's teaching about wives submitting to their husbands, and husbands loving their wives. Even without reading the Scriptures, we have concepts about these matters. Instead of taking Paul's word in Colossians for granted, we should dig into this book in order to discover for ourselves all these aspects of Christ. Then we need to praise the Lord and worship Him according to these aspects. We should say, "Lord, I worship You that You are the portion of the saints. I praise You that You are the image of the invisible God." How good to worship the Lord in this way!

If we know Christ in all these aspects, the praise we offer at the Lord's table meeting will be uplifted. I have been attending the meeting for the Lord's table for more than forty-seven years, and in all these meetings I have listened to the saints praising the Lord. Most of the praises have been on an elementary level. For example, in meeting after meeting the saints may praise the Lord for the blood. This certainly is not wrong. But if we remain on this level, our praise will be shallow. We need to remember the Lord and to praise Him according to the revelation contained in the book of Colossians. We need to use expressions such as those in this stanza from hymn #189 in the hymnal:

Thou art the Son beloved,
  The image of our God;
Thou art the saints' dear portion,
  Imparted through Thy blood.
Among all God's creation
  Thou art the firstborn One;
By thee all was created,
  All for thyself to own.

At the Lord's table we need to remember the Lord as the portion of the saints, as the image of God, as the mystery of God's economy, and as the reality of all positive things. May the Lord enrich our praise!

A. The Processed God

The all-inclusive Christ who indwells us is the processed God (John 14:8-11, 16-20; Matt. 28:19). He has been processed through incarnation, human living, crucifixion, and resurrection, and now He is in ascension.

B. The Life-giving Spirit

As we have pointed out repeatedly, the indwelling Christ is also the life-giving Spirit (1 Cor. 15:45). This Spirit, the all-inclusive Spirit with the bountiful supply (Phil. 1:19), is also the compound Spirit. In Exodus 30:23-30 we have a picture of this compound Spirit. According to this portion of the Word, the holy anointing oil was made by blending four spices with olive oil. Together the spices and the oil formed a compound, an ointment used to anoint the priests, the tabernacle, and everything related to the tabernacle. The oil typifies the Spirit of God, and the four spices typify Christ in His divinity and His humanity with the effectiveness of His death and the power of His resurrection. The compound Spirit typified by the ointment is the very Spirit spoken of in John 7:39. At the time of John 7:39, the compound Spirit was "not yet" because Jesus had not yet been glorified. Now, after the glorification of Christ, the Spirit is no longer simply the Spirit of God; He is the compound Spirit, the Spirit of God compounded with Christ's humanity, the effectiveness of His death, and the power of His resurrection. As the processed

God, Christ is such a compound, all-inclusive, life-giving Spirit.

C. Dwelling in Our Spirit

Christ now dwells in our spirit (2 Tim. 4:22) to be one spirit with us (1 Cor. 6:17). As the life-giving Spirit mingled with our spirit, He is our life and our person (Col. 3:4; Eph. 3:17).

XI. THE HOPE OF GLORY

In 1:27 Paul says not only that Christ dwells within us, but also that He dwells within us as our hope of glory. Christ can be our hope of glory because He dwells in our spirit to be our life and our person. According to 3:4, when Christ our life is manifested, we also shall be manifested with Him in glory. He will appear to be glorified in our redeemed and transfigured body (Rom. 8:23; Phil. 3:21; 2 Thes. 1:10). When Christ comes, we shall be glorified in Him, and He will be glorified in us. This indicates that the indwelling Christ will saturate our entire being, including our physical body. This will cause our body to be transfigured and to become like His glorious body. At that time Christ will be glorified in us. This is Christ in us as the hope of glory.

LIFE-STUDY OF COLOSSIANS

MESSAGE SIXTEEN

PRESENTING EVERY MAN FULL-GROWN IN CHRIST

Scripture Reading: Col. 1:25-28; 2:4, 9; 3:4a; Eph. 3:8-11, 4; 1:23; John 6:57b; 14:19b; Gal. 2:20a; Eph. 4:15, 13b

Speaking of Christ who dwells in us as the hope of glory, Paul says in 1:28, "Whom we announce, warning every man and teaching every man in all wisdom, that we may present every man full-grown in Christ." The Greek word rendered full-grown may also be translated mature, complete, or perfect. Paul's ministry was to impart Christ to others so that they may be perfect and complete by maturing in Christ unto full growth. However, many Christian workers today do not have any concept of presenting every man full-grown in Christ. The goal of their work is something other than this. But we must have the same goal that Paul had.

Even in preaching the gospel, our aim should be to impart life in order to present others mature, full-grown, in Christ. As we preach the gospel to unbelievers, minister Christ to them, and help them to receive the Lord, our goal is not merely that they should be saved from the lake of fire and from God's condemnation. Our goal is not only for them to experience God's forgiveness; it is to minister Christ into them so that they may eventually be presented full-grown in Christ. If we fail to impart Christ to others as we preach the gospel, our gospel preaching will fall short of God's standard. Christ must be infused into all those to whom we speak. Imparting Christ should be our aim in our gospel preaching.

We should have the same goal in our fellowship with the saints. As we contact the saints, our goal should be to minister Christ into them so that they may mature in Him.

Let us now consider several matters related to presenting others mature in Christ.

I. BY MINISTERING CHRIST AS THE PORTION OF THE SAINTS

If we would present others full-grown in Christ, we must minister Christ to them as the portion of the saints (1:12). The Christ we minister must be the all-inclusive One, the centrality and universality of God's economy (1:15, 18-19, 27; 2:4, 9, 16-17; 3:4, 11). If we do not experience Christ in a full way, we shall find it difficult to minister Christ to others. For example, if we do not experience living by Christ, we cannot help anyone else to live by Christ. But if in our daily living we live Christ, grow Christ, and produce Christ, we shall spontaneously infuse Christ into others as we contact them. The more we take Christ as our life and our person, the more we shall be able to minister Christ to others. Having become those who experience Christ and live by Him, we shall influence others to do the same. We need to enjoy Christ as our good land, labor on Him, live in Him, walk in Him, and have our being in Him. If we are such persons, we shall transfuse into others the very Christ whom we experience and by whom we live. In the Lord's recovery what we need is not simply more labor to bring others into the church life. We need to minister the riches of Christ into others so that they may grow and mature. For this we ourselves need to experience more of Christ as the portion of the saints.

II. BY MINISTERING THE UNSEARCHABLE RICHES OF CHRIST FOR THE BUILDING UP OF THE CHURCH

Secondly, to present every man full-grown in Christ, we need to minister the unsearchable riches of Christ for the building up of the church to fulfill God's eternal purpose (Eph. 3:8-11). It is possible to be what everyone would consider a good brother or sister, but still be short of the riches of Christ. In my contact with saints as I have traveled, I have met many who lacked the riches of Christ in their daily living, although everyone would consider them very good brothers and sisters. May the Lord awaken within us the aspiration to be rich in Christ. We need to pray, "Lord, I don't want to be one who seems to be good, but who is poor as far as the riches of Christ are concerned. Lord, for the building up of the church, cause me to be filled with the riches of Christ."

I thank the Lord for those saints whose living is characterized by the riches of Christ. Such brothers and sisters are transparent. Those who are short of the riches of Christ, on the contrary, are opaque, altogether lacking in transparency. But those who have the riches of Christ are crystal clear. Whenever you bring something to them in fellowship, the matter becomes clear to you because they themselves are so transparent. Those who enjoy the riches of Christ become clear as crystal. The more we experience the riches of Christ, the more transparent we shall become. May we all desire to be those who are rich in Christ and fully transparent! May we pray, "Lord, make me a member of the Body who is rich in Your life and who is transparent. Save me from being a member who is good, but who is short of Christ."

Only those who are rich in Christ can build up the Body for the fulfillment of God's eternal purpose. We must admit that we still do not have very much building among us. We may be more concerned about our individual spirituality and growth than about the building up of the church. If we are short of Christ and lacking in transparency, we shall have little concern for the building up of the church. But if we are filled with the riches of Christ and thereby become transparent, we shall be deeply concerned for the building up of the church so that God's purpose may be fulfilled.

III. BY COMPLETING THE WORD OF GOD

We present others full-grown in Christ by completing the Word of God with the full revelation of Christ and the church (1:25-27). To present others mature in Christ we must help them to have the completion of the Word of God concerning Christ as the mystery of God and the church as the mystery of Christ. However, if we consider our situation, we shall realize that not many of us are able to complete the Word in this way. For this reason I am burdened that we would be stirred up to pursue the Lord. We need to hunger and thirst after Him, to pursue Him until we are filled with His riches. We need to pray, "Lord Jesus, we don't want to be indifferent or lukewarm. We long to be absolute with You and to seek You to the uttermost." If we pursue the Lord in such a way, we shall see more regarding Christ and the church. But if we continue to be short of the riches of Christ, we shall not have in our own experience the completion of the Word of God. Hence, there is the desperate need for us to pray and to labor on Christ for the completing of the Word of God concerning Christ and the church.

IV. BY MINISTERING CHRIST AS THE MYSTERY OF GOD

Fourthly, we need to minister Christ as the mystery of God, that is, as the embodiment of God (2:2, 9). We need to share with others from our experience how Christ is the embodiment of the Triune God. We need to be able to testify how we daily experience Christ as the Father, Son, and Spirit. Because we have Christ, we also have the Father. Because we are in Christ, we are also in the Spirit. The Spirit who moves within us actually is Christ Himself. Day by day we should be one spirit with the Lord and experience His being one with us (1 Cor. 6:17). More and more our experience must be that in every aspect of our daily living, wherever we may be, we are one spirit with the Lord. This should not be a doctrine or theory; it must be our practical Christian living.

Concerning my ministry, I often pray like this: "Lord, give me the grace to be one spirit with You as I speak. Lord, I pray that You will speak in my speaking. I believe, Lord, that You are one Spirit with me. But I ask that as I minister the Word I shall be one spirit with You." Whatever impact this ministry has comes from such a oneness with the Lord.

The Lord is the embodiment of the Triune God. This means that all the riches of the Father are embodied in the Son. Furthermore, the Son is realized in a full way as the Spirit, who is now one spirit with us. As Paul says in 1 Corinthians 6:17, "He that is joined unto the Lord is one spirit." The matter of being one spirit with the Lord should not be a mere doctrine to us. On the contrary, it must be our daily, practical experience. In our experience we must know what it is to be one spirit with the Lord, who is the embodiment of the Triune God. If we experience Christ as the embodiment of God, we shall be able to minister Christ to others for their nourishment and enrichment. As we minister Christ to others in this way, they will grow in Him. Growth comes by eating. If others feed on the Christ we minister to them as the mystery of God, they will be perfected and mature in Christ.

V. BY MINISTERING THE CHURCH AS THE MYSTERY OF CHRIST

If we would present others mature in Christ, we must minister the church as the mystery of Christ, as the ex- pension of Christ (Eph. 3:4; 1:23). In his subtlety, Satan has caused many seeking Christians to avoid the matter of the church.

My experience with Brother T. Austin-Sparks illustrates how persistently some avoid the church matter. At our invitation, he came to Taiwan in 1955. We had a wonderful time together as he ministered on Christ. He could clearly echo what we had seen about Christ. In 1957 he came to Taiwan a second time. On this visit he touched the church ground, the standing of the church, in a negative way. In 1958 I accepted his invitation to visit him in England. During the days we were together, we had many long conversations about the church. However, he could not change my mind, and I could not change his concept. He tried his best to avoid the subject of the church, but my concept was that we must labor for the building up of the churches. His intention was to convince us that we should give up the ground of the church. But I pointed out to him that it was impossible for us to have the church practically without the ground of the church. Brother Sparks tried to assure me that he was not opposed to the church. He went on to tell me that during the early years of his ministry, he was invited to speak in Edinburgh. When he spoke about

Christ, the meeting hall was crowded, and the audience was responsive. But when he spoke about the church, the number of people decreased. This caused him to feel that it was not profitable for him to speak on the church.

I went on to ask Brother Sparks how we could practice the principles we both had seen concerning the Lord's Body. He admitted that these principles could not be put into practice in the denominations. But he would not admit that they could be put into practice only on the proper ground of the church. Instead, he emphasized the fact that the church can be produced only by much prayer and through the Spirit. Then I said to him, "Do you think that so many churches on the island of Taiwan did not all come into existence by prayer and through the Spirit?" I asked him what a group of saints should do after they had prayed regarding the church. Still he would not admit that they should take the standing of the church on the ground of oneness. He simply said that they needed to be assured that any move they made was of the Spirit. This was the conclusion of our conversation about the church.

I tried my best to convince him concerning the church, and he tried his best to avoid the church. Eventually, neither of us would change our position.

Today a battle is raging over the church as the expression of Christ. Due to the subtlety of the enemy, most Christian bookstores will sell Brother Nee's books on spirituality, but not his books on the church. Christians, however, cannot become full-grown without the church life. Brother Nee's books related to spiritual matters have been popular with Christians around the world for many years. But the popularity of these books has not caused the condition of Christianity to improve very much. Without the church life, the help people received from Brother Nee's books would eventually leak away because the church life is the only proper vessel to preserve this help. For some, the spiritual books by Brother Nee for the most part supply new doctrinal concepts. Not much is gained for the fulfillment of God's purpose. Does the Lord want people who only seek after spirituality, but who do not participate in the proper church life? Certainly not! Apart from the church,

God's purpose cannot be fulfilled. Because we realize this, the Lord's burden concerning the church presses heavily upon us. We need to practice the church life for the fulfillment of God's eternal purpose. We also need to be faithful to minister the church as the mystery of Christ, as the very expression of Christ.

The Lord's desire is to have the Body, the church. He does not want the church in terminology—He wants the church in practicality. In order for the church life to be practical, there must be local churches. This is made clear in *The Practical Expression of the Church.* Today the practical expression of the church can only be in the local churches. Oh, may we all learn to minister the church as the mystery of Christ, as His expression, in order that others may be presented full-grown in Christ!

Some have claimed that the ministry concerning the church has no future because the opposition against it is so widespread and intense. Certainly if this ministry is simply the work of man, it has no future. But if this ministry is the ministry in the Lord's recovery, the future will be bright. The more others advise us not to minister on the church, the more we must be faithful to minister regarding it. We must be bold and faithful to speak not only of Christ, the Head, but also of the church, His Body. We must not follow today's Christianity. On the contrary, we must follow the pure Word to minister the church as the mystery of Christ.

VI. BY MINISTERING CHRIST AS LIFE TO HIS MEMBERS

Finally, we need to minister Christ as life to His members so that they may live by Him and grow with Him unto maturity. Colossians 3:4 says that Christ is our life, and in John 6:57; 14:19; and Galatians 2:20 we see that we need to live by Him. Then we shall grow with Him unto maturity (Eph. 4:15, 13).

If we desire to present others full-grown in Christ, we must minister to them all the matters we have considered in this message. What a great need there is for the believers to be infused with all the things related to God's economy! If we are faithful to minister these crucial points, we shall be able to present others full-grown in Christ.

LIFE-STUDY OF COLOSSIANS

MESSAGE SEVENTEEN

STRUGGLING ACCORDING TO THE OPERATION OF CHRIST

Scripture Reading: Col. 1:28-29; 2:1-2; Eph. 3:20; 1:19-22

In this message we shall consider the matter of struggling according to the operation of Christ (1:29). We have pointed out that Paul labored to present every man full-grown in Christ. Presenting others full-grown in Christ is a very difficult task, a task which can be accomplished only by struggling according to Christ's operation.

THE PRINCIPLE ORDAINED BY GOD

Some may think that the way to present others full-grown in Christ is to pray. However, it is possible to have a superstitious understanding of prayer. For example, suppose someone thinks that meals can be prepared only by prayer and that there is no need to go shopping or to cook food. Such a concept is superstitious. In presenting others full-grown in Christ we need to follow the principle set up in Genesis 2: Man tills the ground, and God sends the rain (v. 5). On the one hand, we must till the ground. On the other hand, only God can send the rain. As we trust in God and look to Him for the rain, we should be faithful in our responsibility to till the ground. This means that we must fulfill the principle ordained by God. If we depend only on our work of tilling the ground and do not trust in the Lord to send the rain, we are wrong. But we are also wrong if we only pray to the Lord for rain and do not fulfill our responsibility to till the ground. Applying this principle to the matter of presenting every man full-grown in Christ, we see that we should not merely pray, but also labor according to Christ's operation.

STRUGGLING FOR THE HEARTS TO BE COMFORTED

In 2:1 Paul says, "For I want you to know how great a struggle I have for you, and for those in Laodicea, and for as many as have not seen my face in the flesh." This verse indicates that Paul was struggling, agonizing, wrestling, to see a particular matter accomplished among the Colossians and Laodiceans. Verse 2 shows the object of Paul's struggle: "That their hearts may be comforted, being knit together in love and unto all riches of the full assurance of understanding, unto the full knowledge of the mystery of God, Christ." For years I could not understand why Paul spoke about hearts being comforted immediately after giving such a high vision of Christ. Not knowing how to connect the vision in chapter one to this word in chapter two, I spent a great deal of time to find out why such a word was inserted. Paul did not say that he struggled so that the Colossians and Laodiceans would see the vision of Christ given in chapter one. According to my concept, this is what he should have said. If verse 2 had been written in this way, it would have been much easier for me to understand. Nevertheless, Paul did not say that he struggled so that the saints would exercise their spirits to see what he had shared with them concerning Christ. He struggled that their hearts might be comforted.

Why was it necessary for the hearts of the Colossians to be comforted, knit together in love and unto all riches of the full assurance of understanding? It took years before I could answer this question. Assurance implies two things: faith and knowledge. When we have faith and knowledge, we have certainty about what we believe. This certainty then becomes our assurance. Paul wrestled so that the hearts of the Colossians would have full assurance.

The words "unto the full knowledge of the mystery of God, Christ" are in apposition to "unto all riches of the full assurance of understanding." The second "unto" equals the first. Although I could understand certain of these details, I could not understand the verse as a whole. I simply did not know the reason for this word.

We thank the Lord that, through the years, He has shown us the reason. As we consider this reason, let us recall that, as sister books, Ephesians is concerned with the church as the Body, whereas Colossians deals with Christ as the Head. Ephesians places great emphasis on the human spirit; it uses the phrase "in spirit" repeatedly. Colossians, however, refers to the human spirit only once (2:5). In Colossians the heart is of crucial significance. Here Paul emphasizes the importance of the heart in receiving the revelation concerning Christ. For years we have spoken about turning to the spirit, exercising the spirit, and abiding in the spirit. However, we have not given as much attention to taking care of the heart. Paul knew that if we would present others full-grown in Christ, we must be concerned about the condition of their hearts. The fact that he concludes chapter one with a word about presenting every man mature in Christ and opens chapter two with a word about the comforting of the hearts indicates that presenting others full-grown in the Lord has much to do with the heart.

Because of the different observances, ordinances, and philosophies that had crept into the church life, the hearts of the saints in Colosse had been hurt; they had become cold and dissatisfied. Whenever such things come in, the result is always dissension and division. We must guard the door of the church lest such things enter in and cause harm. The church in Colosse had been invaded by Jewish ordinances and observances and by pagan philosophy, mysticism, and asceticism. These things caused the saints to become opinionated, dissenting, and dissatisfied. They also caused the hearts of the saints to be hurt and to become cold, divided, and separated from one another. Therefore, Paul struggled on behalf of the saints that their hearts would be comforted and knit together in love.

In this verse to be comforted means to be cherished, that is, to be lovingly warmed up. Ephesians 5:29 says that Christ nourishes and cherishes His church. To nourish is to feed, and to cherish is to make warm. How the saints in Colosse needed the Lord's cherishing! Their hearts needed to be comforted, to be warmed.

Paul speaks of the hearts being knit together in love. The words "knit together in love" indicate that some kind of separation had taken place and that there had been a loss of love. The different observances, ordinances, and philosophies that had crept in had caused this loss of love.

THE HEART AND THE MIND

In this verse Paul deals with two crucial organs of our inner being: the heart and the mind. (The word understanding implies the mind.) Once the heart has been hurt and has become cold and divided, it is easy for the mind to be distracted or even attacked by the enemy. When the mind is in such a condition, it cannot understand the word that is ministered concerning Christ and God's economy.

Problems in the heart are often the cause of mental problems. If a person's mind is under attack by the enemy, this is an indication that his heart is wrong in some way. Whenever the heart is wrong, it is easy for the mind to be in darkness or subject to attack. This is an important principle. Most cases of mental illness have their source in problems that exist in the heart. More than forty years ago, the superintendent of a large mental hospital told me that, according to his experience and observation, mental problems are caused by problems related to greed for money and sex. These are problems of the heart. Greed for money causes problems in the hearts of some, whereas lust causes problems in the hearts of others. Such problems cause the mind to come under attack. Through years of experience, we have learned that mental illness can be traced to problems in the heart. The mind is attacked because the heart is wrong. Perhaps someone has a certain ambition or desire in his heart. If this ambition or desire is not fulfilled and is not dealt with, the mind may be attacked.

Paul no doubt realized this; he knew that it was crucial for the hearts of the Colossians to be comforted and knit together in love. If their hearts were cared for in a proper way, the saints would have the riches of the full assurance of understanding. Their minds would once again function normally to understand spiritual things. When our hearts are comforted, our minds will function properly. But if there is a problem in our heart, there will be a problem in our mind also. The heart regulates the mind. Whether the mind is normal or abnormal depends on the condition of the heart.

The relationship with the saints in the church life tests what is in our hearts. If our hearts are possessed by certain ambitions, desires, and goals, our minds will not be normal and will cause us to have problems with others. For example, if my mind is under attack because of a problem in my heart, I may be very displeased if a brother does not greet me with a smile. I may be further troubled if this same brother invites another brother to lunch with him, but does not invite me. I may become quite angry over the situation. This anger is not caused by temper; it is caused by the problem in my heart. In my heart I may desire respect, honor, and position. This may cause me to feel that others should show respect for me by greeting me in a pleasant way. However, if I have no problem in my heart, I shall not be troubled if a brother does not smile at me or does not include me in a certain activity. If our heart is right, we shall be happy in the church life, no matter what happens to us. But if there is a problem in our heart, we shall be displeased with the church. This is a very serious matter.

FULL ASSURANCE OF UNDERSTANDING

For the heart to be knit together with others in love involves the emotion, whereas to have the riches of the full assurance of the understanding involves the mind. If we do not have a proper heart, we shall not be able to receive the revelation concerning Christ. To see the vision of Christ we need a heart that is comforted, cherished, and knit together with others in love and unto all the riches of the full assurance of understanding. How happy I am that the hearts of the saints in the Lord's recovery have been comforted and knit together! Because our hearts have been knit together in love and unto all riches of the full assurance of understanding, we can receive the revelation in the book of Colossians.

The riches of the full assurance of understanding equal the full knowledge of the mystery of God, Christ. When our hearts have been comforted and our minds function normally, we shall have the full knowledge of Christ as the mystery of God.

Now we can see why Paul struggled for the hearts of the Colossians to be comforted. He knew that this is the only way the saints can have the full assurance of understanding. Because our hearts have been cherished and knit together, we in the Lord's recovery have such an assurance. This assurance gives us the full knowledge of Christ as the mystery of God. May the Lord daily cherish our hearts that we may have a healthy church life! When our hearts are happy, it seems that all the brothers and sisters are wonderful. But when our hearts are not happy, the opposite seems to be the case. How important it is for our hearts to be cherished by the Lord!

THE FIRST STEP IN PRESENTING OTHERS FULL-GROWN IN CHRIST

Only after their hearts had been comforted could the Colossians receive the revelation concerning Christ. Because this matter is so important, this book emphasizes the heart instead of the spirit. We cannot present others full-grown in Christ unless their hearts have been comforted. If their hearts have not been cherished, they will not be able to receive anything we minister to them concerning Christ. Therefore, the first step in presenting others full-grown in Christ is to comfort their hearts unto all the riches of the full assurance of understanding. Especially the leading ones should look to the Lord for the grace to be able to comfort all the distracted, dissatisfied, and disappointed hearts. When the hearts of the saints have been comforted, it will be easy for us to minister the riches of Christ to them. But if the saints have problems in their hearts, they will have trouble with their minds. The only way to solve the problems in the mind is for the hearts to be adjusted through the Lord's cherishing. This is a crucial lesson for us all to learn.

PAUL'S STRUGGLE

In 1:29 Paul said that he struggled according to Christ's operation within him. This struggle was his labor to present every man full-grown in Christ. He endeavored to do this by announcing Christ, by warning every man, and by teaching every man in all wisdom.

CHRIST'S OPERATION

According to 1:29, the operation of Christ operates in us in power. There is a difference between Christ operating in us and Christ's operation operating in us. Because Christ as the hope of glory operates in us, there is an operation which also operates in us. Christ Himself operates in us. But Christ operating in us causes an operation which also operates in us. This operation operates in us in power.

Every saved person has at least some experience of Christ's operation. To be saved is not merely to have our sins forgiven and to be justified by God. It is also to have Christ imparted into us. The Christ who dwells in us also operates in us. As we have pointed out, His operating becomes the operation that operates in us. Paul's struggling for the saints was according to this operation.

Some saints may feel that they sense very little of Christ's operation within them. The reason for this lack is the shortage of prayer. We need to go to the Lord with a repentant heart and say, "Lord, I am still so natural, so much in the self and in the old man. Lord, forgive me and cleanse me with Your precious blood. Lord, I desire to be enlightened, purified, and made transparent. I ask You to show me what You want of me. Expose me so that I may be filled with You." If we pray in this way, Christ's operation will have a way to operate within us.

I can testify that I am energized by Christ's operation. The more I pray, the more His operation energizes me. However, if

I fail to pray, I would become cold and quiet. The reason you may sense little of Christ's operation within you is that you strive too much and pray too little to contact the Lord. By opening to the Lord in prayer, you give ground for Christ's operation to operate within you. Then you will be able to struggle according to this operation to present others mature in Christ.

Christ's operation operates in power. Paul refers to this power in Ephesians 3:7 and 20. In Ephesians 3:7 he speaks of "the operation of His power," and in 3:20, of the "power which operates in us." This power is the power of resurrection life (Phil. 3:10) within the believers (Eph. 1:19). It is the very power that operated in Christ to raise Him from the dead, to seat Him at God's right hand in the heavenlies, and to subject all things under His feet (Eph. 1:20-22). Hence, this power is the resurrection power, the transcending power, and the subduing power. According to Christ's operation in such a power, we may struggle to present others full-grown in Christ.

What Paul did in struggling to present others full-grown in Christ is an example which serves for the perfecting of the saints for the building up of the Body of Christ. It is to struggle according to the operation of Christ that operates in us, that is, to labor by the resurrecting, transcending, and subduing power within us.

LIFE-STUDY OF COLOSSIANS

MESSAGE EIGHTEEN

CHRIST—THE MYSTERY OF GOD

Scripture Reading: Col. 2:2-3, 9; 1:19

At the end of 2:2 Paul speaks of the "full knowledge of the mystery of God, Christ." The book of Ephesians is on the mystery of Christ, which is the church, the Body (Eph. 3:4). This book is on the mystery of God, which is Christ, the Head. It is crucial that we know Christ not only as our Savior and Lord, but also as the mystery of God.

All Christians love the Lord Jesus. The only difference among them in this matter is the degree of their love for Him. Even a backsliding believer loves the Lord to a certain extent. How much we love the Lord depends on how much we know Him and how much we realize concerning Him. For example, a child may appreciate a little box made to contain a diamond ring more than the ring itself. This shows that the degree of love is determined by the degree of appreciation. The more we know the Lord Jesus and appreciate Him, the more we shall love Him. Hence, we need to go on to know the Lord Jesus not only as our Savior and Lord, but also as the mystery of God.

If we would know Christ as the mystery of God, we need to have the full experience of everything covered in 2:2. In this verse Paul says, "That their hearts may be comforted, being knit together in love and unto all riches of the full assurance of understanding, unto the full knowledge of the mystery of God, Christ." The word "unto" means "resulting in." If the hearts of the Colossians were comforted and knit together in love, the result would be all the riches of the full assurance of understanding, an understanding no doubt related to the mystery of God, Christ.

THE NEED TO EXERCISE OUR WHOLE BEING

We cannot contact the Lord or know Him as God's mystery without exercising our spirit. As we shall see, our whole being needs to be exercised. Every aspect of man's being—spirit, soul, and body—is complicated. If you spend time examining your face in a mirror, you will be impressed with the complexity of your physical body. Human beings are not simple organisms. In our soul we have the mind, the emotion, and the will. Furthermore, in our spirit we have the conscience, the intuition, and the fellowship. Every part of our complex being must be exercised to receive the revelation of Christ as the mystery of God.

God Himself is a mystery, and Christ is the mystery of this mystery. Surely we cannot fathom such a mystery simply by reading the letter of the Scriptures. Since Christ dwells in our spirit, we need to exercise our spirit in order to know Him as the mystery of God. Never regard Christ as a mere object to be known in an outward way. As the crucified and resurrected One, He is living both on the throne in the heavens and in our spirit as well. Hence, it is of utmost importance that we exercise our spirit to contact Him. This means that we must open up from the depths of our being and call on Him. Our spirit is our deepest part, deeper than the heart and all the parts of the soul. There fore, to exercise our spirit is to open the deepest part of our being to call on the name of the Lord Jesus and to contact Him as the living One within us.

We are complex, but Christ is far more complex. To know Him, we must not only exercise our spirit, but also have our heart comforted. This means that our heart must be cherished, warmed. Moreover, our mind must be sober, our emotion must be regulated, and our will must be subdued. Every part of our inner being must be proper and function in a normal way. This is the reason Paul speaks of the hearts being comforted in relation to having the full knowledge of Christ as the mystery of God.

In 2:2 Paul goes on to speak of all the riches of the full assurance of understanding. The comforting of the heart must have a result. In this case the result is having all the riches of the full assurance of understanding. We need to have such an assurance, for example, concerning the ground of the church. Some saints claim to know the church ground and to be committed to it. However, they are actually quite wishy-washy and have no certainty related to the ground of the church. They have faith, but they do not have the certainty which gives us full assurance.

Allow me to testify of my experience about becoming assured regarding the ground of the church. In 1932 we began to practice the church life in Chefoo, my hometown. After several months, opposition rose up against us. Before we began to practice the church life, I was loved and respected by the Christian leaders in that city. They regarded me as one who was for the Lord Jesus in an absolute way. However, the attitude of those leaders toward me began to change when more and more of the promising ones began to come into the church. This troubled those Christian leaders, and negative rumors were circulated about us. Furthermore, those who once respected me no longer greeted me when they saw me on the street. Deeply concerned about this, I went to the Lord and inquired about the situation. I asked Him to show me what was wrong. I spent more than a month thoroughly considering the matter before the Lord. Eventually I concluded that if I were to be a man, I had to believe in the Lord Jesus; that if I were to believe in the Lord, I had to love Him; and that if I were to love Him, I had to take the way of the church. As a result, I received the full assurance concerning the ground of the church. I had not only faith, but also the knowledge which caused me to have certainty. For more than forty-six years I have not changed my position with respect to the church ground, no matter how much I have suffered because of the stand I have taken. Some co-workers who used to be close to me betrayed me because they were afraid to face opposition regarding the church ground. Some of them had even given messages on the ground of the church. But actually they were wishy-washy. They did not have the full assurance of understanding that Paul speaks of in 2:2. Paul realized that concerning the mystery of God, Christ, the believers needed certainty, the assurance that comes from faith and knowledge. Those who have such an assurance are not wishy-washy in this matter.

After making my decision about the ground of the church, I spent some time with Brother Nee in Shanghai during a period of turmoil. Attempting to comfort him, I said, "Brother Nee, I am one with you because you are taking the Lord's way. I assure you, even if you turn from this way, I will not change my mind. I have the full assurance concerning the Lord's way in the church." This is the full assurance of understanding that Paul speaks of in 2:2. Concerning Christ as the mystery of God, we need faith, knowledge, certainty, and thorough understanding.

The Colossians did not have the full assurance concerning Christ. Otherwise, they would not have turned to the worship of angels or taken in such things as observances, ordinances, and philosophies. On the one hand, they had received Christ and knew something about Him. On the other hand, their knowledge of Christ was not with the full assurance of understanding. The Colossians definitely believed in the Lord Jesus and held to the faith. But they did not have all the riches of the full assurance of understanding. They knew that Christ was the Son of God, and they had received Him. However, because they were rather wishy-washy, they also accepted various observeances, ordinances, and philosophies.

If we would have all the riches of the full assurance of understanding concerning Christ as the mystery of God, every part of our being must be exercised. We should not be wishy-washy in any way. I am concerned for those in the Lord's recovery who have never exercised themselves in a full way. Due to this lack of exercise, they may not have the full assurance of understanding concerning the recovery.

Certain ones were with us for years. While they were with us, they praised the Lord for His recovery and declared that they were absolutely for the church life. But they eventually turned against the recovery and even condemned it. The reason for such a change is that they never had a thorough exercise concerning the Lord's recovery and never received the full assurance of understanding regarding it.

How much we need to be exercised to know Christ as the mystery of God! We should be able to say, "Lord Jesus, apart from You I have no heart for anything. Lord, my mind, will, and emotion are absolutely for You. I know what I believe, and I know what I am doing in Your recovery. I am willing to lay down my life for You. If I had ten lives, I would give every one of them for the recovery. Every fiber of my being, Lord, is for You." If you exercise your whole being in this way, you will have the full assurance of understanding. You will not have any doubt about what you are doing or about the way you are taking. You will have the kind of assurance martyrs have when they lay down their lives for the Lord.

ALL THE RICHES OF THE FULL ASSURANCE OF UNDERSTANDING

In 2:2 Paul speaks not only of the full assurance, but of all the riches of the full assurance of understanding. As we consider this, let us once again use the ground of the church as an example. Some saints may have the full assurance concerning the church ground, but they may not have the riches in their understanding. When they speak about the ground of the church, they have little to say. The reason for this is the lack of the riches in their understanding. If we have the riches of the full assurance of understanding with respect to the truth of the ground of oneness, we shall have much to say concerning it. Regarding the ground of the church, we need to be exercised until we have all the riches of the full assurance of understanding.

The principle is the same with knowing Christ as the mystery of God. We need to be exercised to such an extent that we always have something to say about Christ as the mystery of God. How inexhaustible Christ is! If we have all the riches of the full assurance of understanding concerning Him, we shall never be short of things to say about Him. The riches of understanding will give us rich utterance.

I wish to emphasize again and again that such riches only

come through the exercise of our inner being. In particular, we need to exercise our understanding in studying the Bible. Do not study the Word in a superficial way, and do not take things for granted. Instead, exercise yourself over every phrase, sometimes even over every word. For example, in 1:12 Paul speaks of the portion of the saints in the light. We need to ask why he uses the phrase "in the light." We need to inquire of the Lord and dig into the Word until we have the riches of the full assurance of understanding. To know Christ as the embodiment of God requires such an exercise of our being.

As we exercise over the Word, we shall receive light. For instance, we may exercise over the matter of the comforting of the hearts in 2:2. Eventually, we shall be enlightened. I repeat, our whole being—our spirit, heart, soul, mind, emotion, and will—must be exercised in the Word. Then we shall love the Lord with our whole being and have all the riches of the full assurance of understanding concerning Christ as the mystery of God.

THE TREASURES OF WISDOM AND KNOWLEDGE HIDDEN IN CHRIST

Concerning Christ as the mystery of God, Paul says, "In Whom are all the treasures of wisdom and knowledge hidden" (2:3). According to history, the influence of Gnostic teaching, implying Greek philosophy, invaded the Gentile churches in Paul's time. Hence, Paul told the Colossians that all the treasures of real wisdom and knowledge are hidden in Christ. This is the spiritual wisdom and knowledge of the divine economy concerning Christ and the church. Wisdom is related to our spirit, and knowledge is related to our mind (Eph. 1:8, 17).

God is the unique source of wisdom and knowledge. All the treasures of wisdom and knowledge are hidden in the very Christ who is the mystery of God. Because the church at Colosse had been invaded by pagan philosophy, Paul was helping the Colossians trace wisdom and knowledge to their true source in God. Christ is the mystery of God, who alone is the source of all wisdom and knowledge. It seems as if Paul wanted to say, "Colossians, since you have received the Christ in whom all the treasures of wisdom and knowledge are hidden, why do you still need philosophy? Why do you accept the teaching of Gnosticism? You do this because you do not have the full assurance concerning what you believe. You have faith, but you don't have certainty." Paul knew that the hearts of the Colossians needed to be comforted and knit together in love so that they could have all the riches of the full assurance of understanding. If they had such an assurance, they would know all the treasures of wisdom and knowledge that are hidden in Christ.

The fact that wisdom and knowledge are embodied in Christ is proved by His spoken words, especially those recorded in the Gospels of Matthew and John. In these books, the Lord spoke about the kingdom and about life. The Lord's words recorded in these books contain the highest philosophy. None of the teachings of the philosophers, including the ethical teachings of Confucius, compare to them. The concept in the Lord's words is too deep and profound. Anyone who makes a thorough study of philosophy will have to admit that the highest philosophy is that found in the teachings of Jesus Christ. Truly all the treasures of wisdom and knowledge are in Him.

If we exercise our being to contact the Lord, Christ as the life-giving Spirit will saturate our spirit and our mind. Then we also shall have in our experience the wisdom and knowledge that are hidden in Christ. In this way we experience Him as the mystery of God. We should not be like the Colossians, who allowed pagan philosophy to defraud them of the wisdom and knowledge hidden in Christ.

THE EMBODIMENT OF THE FULLNESS OF THE GODHEAD

As the mystery of God, Christ is also the embodiment of the fullness of the Godhead. In 1:19 Paul says, "For in Him all the fullness was pleased to dwell." Then in 2:9 he says, "For in Him dwells all the fullness of the Godhead bodily."

Fullness in these verses refers not to the riches of God, but to the expression of the riches of God. What dwells in Christ is not only the riches of the Godhead, but the expression of the riches of what God is. It is crucial for us to see that the fullness of the Godhead is the expression of the Godhead, that is, the expression of what God is. The Godhead is expressed both in the old creation, the universe, and in the new creation, the church. Notice that both in 1:19 and 2:9 Paul uses the word "all" to describe fullness. All the fullness, all the expression, is in the old creation and in the new creation.

The word Godhead in 2:9 refers to deity, which is different from divinity in Romans 1:20. This reference to deity strongly indicates the deity of Christ. Such a deity is with the fullness of the Godhead versus the tradition of man and the elements of the world.

In 1:19 and in 2:9 we see two aspects of all the fullness. According to 1:19, all the fullness was pleased to dwell in Christ. According to 2:9, all the fullness dwells in Christ bodily. This implies the physical body which Christ put on in His humanity. It indicates that all the fullness of the Godhead dwells in Christ as the One who has a human body. Before His incarnation, the fullness of the Godhead dwelt in Him as the eternal Word, but it did not dwell in Him bodily. After He became incarnate, clothed with a human body, the fullness of the Godhead began to dwell in a bodily way, and in His glorified body (Phil. 3:21) now and forever it dwells.

LIFE-STUDY OF COLOSSIANS

MESSAGE NINETEEN

THE EXPERIENCE OF CHRIST AS THE MYSTERY OF GOD

Scripture Reading: Col. 2:2-9

In this message we come to the matter of the experience of Christ as the mystery of God. We shall consider a number of points which help us experience Christ in this way.

I. TO HAVE THE FULL KNOWLEDGE OF HIM AS THE MYSTERY OF GOD

If we would experience Christ as the mystery of God, we need to have the full knowledge of Him as God's mystery. We have pointed out that Paul struggled for the Colossians that their hearts would be comforted "unto the full knowledge of the mystery of God, Christ" (2:2). In order to have the full knowledge of such a mystery, our whole being needs to be exercised. If we simply believe in Christ without loving Him, we cannot have this knowledge. Likewise, if we love Him partially but not wholly, we cannot have the full knowledge of Him. We need to love the Lord Jesus with our whole being. For this reason, Mark 12:30, quoting Deuteronomy 6:5, says, "Thou shalt love the Lord thy God with all thy heart, and with all thy soul, and with all thy mind, and with all thy strength." When our entire being is exercised to love the Lord Jesus, we shall gain the full knowledge of Him.

Some Christians are fond of the hymn, "Oh, how I love Jesus." However, this hymn may be sung in a superficial way; it is not according to the full knowledge of Christ as the mystery of God. Only by exercising our entire being can we know Christ in this way.

I recommend that all the saints in the Lord's recovery study three crucial books in the New Testament: Matthew,

John, and Hebrews. A number of helpful Life-study Messages have been given on these books. The studies on John and Hebrews are especially thorough. If you spend adequate time on these three books, you will gain a considerable amount of knowledge concerning Christ.

II. TO RECEIVE HIM

In 2:6 Paul says that the Colossians "have received Christ Jesus the Lord." Christ is the portion of the saints (1:12) for our enjoyment. To believe in Him is to receive Him. As the all-inclusive Spirit (2 Cor. 3:17), He enters into us and dwells in our spirit (2 Tim. 4:22) to be everything to us.

Once we have received Christ Jesus, we need not receive Him again. But we must apply what we have received. However, only a very small percentage of those who have received Christ apply Him. We all must practice to apply the living Christ in a practical way day by day. To employ a common term, we need to use Christ. For more than fifty years, I have been learning how to use Christ. I can testify that this is difficult because by birth it is not natural for us to use Christ, nor does our training condition us to use Him. Recently, most of my confession to the Lord has been related to my failure to apply Him. The hardest lesson for us to learn as Christians is to apply Christ and to use Him. We have heard a number of messages on living Christ, growing Christ, and producing Christ. Nevertheless, in our daily living we spontaneously use the self instead of Christ. There is no need for us to try to use the self; we use it automatically and spontaneously.

In the Gospels the Lord charges us to "watch and pray." I have spent a number of years considering this word. At first I thought that this command was not necessary. But eventually I learned that I certainly need to watch and pray, especially in the matter of applying Christ. As we are waking up in the morning, we need to be watchful not to do anything without applying Christ. Often as we wake up early in the morning, it seems that demons are swarming around the headboard of the bed. Although we are protected by the Lord and covered with His prevailing blood, we still need to be watchful and resist the evil thoughts injected into us by the enemy. Do not think about anything without applying Christ. We certainly need to be on the alert; that is, we need to be watchful and to pray. But very few Christians watch and pray in order to apply Christ.

Although we have all received the Lord Jesus, we are very short in using Him, in applying Him. If we fail to apply Him, then in a practical way in our daily living there is little significance to having received Him. Our experience of Christ should not be so superficial, and we should not take so many things for granted. We are thankful for God's salvation in Christ, and we are grateful that we have received Him. But now we must go on to apply the very One we have received.

III. TO BE ROOTED IN HIM

In 2:7 Paul speaks of having been rooted in Christ. To be rooted in Him is for the growth in life. In this verse Paul views the believers as plants who have been rooted in Christ as the soil. However, many Christians have not been rooted in Christ adequately.

If we have been rooted in Christ properly, there will be no need to talk much about the ground of the church. The ground of the church is oneness. But the base of this oneness is the one Spirit, the one Lord, and the one God and Father, as mentioned by Paul in Ephesians 4. If we have been truly rooted in Christ, in our experience He will be the base of our oneness. Some Seventh-Day Adventists consider the keeping of the Sabbath another testimony on earth in addition to the local churches. Such a statement indicates a lack of being rooted in Christ. If we have been rooted in Him deeply and properly, we would never say that God has set up another testimony. God's unique testimony is Jesus Christ. If we have been rooted in Him, nothing will be able to distract us from Him. We all should be able to say, "Lord Jesus, I thank You that I have been rooted in You. I have no standing apart from You." In the Lord's recovery we can testify that our ground is Christ and Christ alone.

If we consider the situation of today's Christianity, we shall see that the various denominations and independent groups have something other than Christ as their ground. The Seventh-Day Adventists have as their ground the keeping of the seventh day, whereas the ground of the Baptist denomination is baptism by immersion. Some denominations, such as the Church of Christ, go so far as to insist that only in their water can a believer be baptized properly. Although some groups insist on baptism by immersion, others oppose it; they claim that baptism is strictly spiritual and in the Spirit.

In 1964 I met a man who argued strongly against baptism in water. He insisted that the baptism spoken of in Romans 6 refers to baptism in the Spirit. He interpreted every New Testament reference to baptism after John the Baptist as baptism in the Spirit. He even became quite angry when his position was challenged according to certain verses. A few days later as I was ministering in a certain place, I was challenged by a woman from the Church of Christ concerning water baptism. Just a few days prior, a man argued with me about baptism in the Spirit. Now a woman boldly asked about water baptism. Neither this man nor this woman had been adequately rooted in Christ. This illustrates the shameful fact that Christians are divided because they take as their ground something other than Christ.

Paul realized the importance of being rooted in Christ. He knew that it was a serious matter to be transplanted from Christ and to be rooted in something else, such as heathen philosophy or Jewish ordinances. He wanted the Colossians to see that philosophy was not the soil in which they had been rooted. They had been rooted in Christ. He is our unique soil.

IV. TO BE BUILT UP IN HIM

Having been rooted in Christ, we now are "being built up in Him" (2:7). To be built up is for the building of the Body. Although we have been rooted, we are still in the process of being built up. This is a corporate matter as well as a personal matter. A building is not composed merely of one item, but of many items that have been fitted together. We need to be rooted in Christ and also built up in the church.

Paul was concerned lest the Colossians be distracted from Christ and the church. They had been rooted in Christ, but they still had to go on to be built up in the church. In order to be built up corporately, the Colossians had to forsake the Judaistic observances and the heathen ordinances and philosophies. Otherwise, they would have been transplanted from Christ and rooted in something else. Furthermore, they would have been led astray from the church life. Whenever we take in some kind of philosophy, ordinance, observance, or practice in place of Christ, the church life is annulled. We are divided from those believers who have different opinions concerning these matters. Those who are preoccupied with such things will eventually cease to care about the church life.

In principle, this is what happened to some saints among us who were influenced by certain concepts. As a result of this influence, they lost their heart for the church life. It was no longer possible for them to be built up in a corporate way. How crucial it is to be rooted in Christ and to be built up in Christ and in the church! In this way we experience Christ as the mystery of God.

V. TO BE ESTABLISHED IN THE FAITH ABOUNDING IN THANKSGIVING

Verse 7 concludes with the words, "Being established in the faith as you were taught, abounding in thanksgiving." The words "in the faith" here mean in our faith, the subjective faith by which we believe. If we are distracted from Christ and turn our attention to things that replace Him, our faith will be weakened, perhaps even shaken. But if we remain in Christ and are built up in the church, our faith will be strengthened.

Those who become dissenting and forsake the church life experience a weakening of their faith. Outwardly they may proclaim to have sweet fellowship with the Lord, but inwardly their faith has waned. When they are alone, they may wonder what is happening inside them. They are troubled by doubts, and they know deep within that they have lost their fellowship with the Lord. Because they have so many doubts and questions, they cannot be established in their faith. By contrast, those who remain in Christ and the church have strong faith and firm assurance.

We have pointed out that "the faith" in verse 7 refers to our faith, the subjective faith. Why does Paul say "the faith" when he is actually speaking of our faith? The answer is that he regards the faith as our faith, and our faith as the faith. We cannot be established in someone else's faith; we must be established in our own faith. This means that our faith must become the faith and that the faith must be ours. We are established in our faith, which is the faith.

The way to be established in the faith is by abounding in thanksgiving. When we are right with the Lord and in fellowship with Him, we are filled with thanksgiving. But when we are not right with the Lord, we are not able to give thanks. If you ask the dissenting ones if they are abounding with thanksgiving, their mouths will be stopped. If we claim to have good fellowship with the Lord but cannot render thanks to Him, then our claim is false.

According to this verse, the words "abounding in thanksgiving" are related to "being established in the faith." This indicates that whether or not we have been established in the faith depends on whether or not we are abounding in thanksgiving. If we do a certain thing in fellowship with the Lord, we shall be filled with thanksgiving. However, if we do anything that is apart from Him, we shall not be able to give thanks. For example, are you able to thank the Lord when you participate in a particular form of worldly entertainment? You may claim to be happy, but you cannot honestly thank the Lord. Sometimes it seems that we can thank the Lord for a certain thing, but after a little while we repent of the very thing for which we have given thanks. We must not deceive ourselves. Instead, we should check if we are abounding in thanksgiving. If we are, then we are being established in the faith.

VI. TO WALK IN HIM

Another way to experience Christ as the mystery of God is to "walk in Him" (2:6). As we have received Christ, we should walk in Him. To walk is to live, to act, to behave, and to have our being. We should walk, live, and act in Christ so that we may enjoy His riches, just as the children of Israel lived in the good land and enjoyed all its rich produce.

In our experience Christ should be the good land in which we live and walk. This should not merely be a doctrine to us. We need to pray, "Lord, I want to live and walk in You. Lord, I pray that You will be the good land to me in my experience, and that every aspect of my living may be in You."

VII. NOT TO BE DELUDED AND CARRIED OFF FROM HIM

In 2:4 Paul says, "This I say that no one may delude you with persuasive speech." In verse 8 he goes on to say, "Beware that no one carries you off as spoil through his philosophy and empty deceit, according to the tradition of men, according to the elements of the world, and not according to Christ." If we would experience Christ as the mystery of God, we must take care not to be deluded or carried off from Him. We should not be led away to anything that replaces Christ. We need to remain in Him. As long as we remain in Christ, we shall also remain in the church. Christ must be our only base, our only ground and standing.

In the past few years some were distracted by certain things which they took as their ground instead of Christ. The issue is not whether these things were right or wrong. It is that they were used as a standing in place of Christ. Christ should be our unique focus. We should not allow anything, even the most correct and scriptural things, to replace Him. If we care for anything instead of Christ, we shall be deluded and carried off from Him and thereby become present-day Colossians. Any who have been deluded and carried away from Christ need to receive Paul's word in this book and return to the all-inclusive Christ. May we all experience Him as the mystery of God!

LIFE-STUDY OF COLOSSIANS

MESSAGE TWENTY

TO WALK IN CHRIST, THE MYSTERY OF GOD

Scripture Reading: Col. 2:6; Deut. 8:7-10; Rom. 8:11; 2 Tim. 4:22; Phil. 1:19; 1 Cor. 6:17; Rom. 8:6, 4; Gal. 5:16, 25

In the previous message we spoke about experiencing Christ as the mystery of God. Now we shall go on to consider how to walk in such a Christ. In 2:6 Paul says, "As therefore you have received Christ Jesus the Lord, walk in Him." To walk in Christ as the mystery of God is to live, act, behave, and have our being in Him.

In chapter one of Colossians Paul presents a profound revelation of Christ. The first aspect of Christ unveiled in this chapter is Christ as the portion of the saints (v. 12). The good land in the Old Testament typifies Christ as the saints' portion or lot. In this chapter Paul also shows that Christ is the image of the invisible God, the firstborn of all creation, the Head of the Body, the firstborn from among the dead, and the One in whom all the fullness is pleased to dwell.

Paul opens chapter two with a word about his great struggle for the Colossians that their hearts would be comforted "unto all riches of the full assurance of understanding, unto the full knowledge of the mystery of God, Christ" (v. 2). Only when the hearts of the saints in Colosse were comforted, cherished, and warmed, could they have a proper understanding of Christ. This would enable them to have the genuine experience of Christ. The Colossians needed a comforted heart and a sober mind in order to have the full knowledge of the Christ they had received and from whom they had been distracted. This Christ, the mystery of God, is the One in whom all the treasures of wisdom and knowledge are hidden (v. 3). Furthermore, He is the One in whom all the fullness of the Godhead dwells bodily (2:9). Once the Colossians had the full assurance of understanding concerning the all-inclusive Christ, they could then walk in Him.

We have pointed out that the word walk in 2:6 means to live, act, behave, and have our being. The One in whom we are to walk is the all-inclusive One who is revealed in a profound way in chapter one. As such a One, Christ is the portion of the saints and the mystery of God's economy. Like the Colossians, we need to be exhorted to walk in the Christ who is everything to us.

OUR GOOD LAND

As Paul was writing this chapter of Colossians, he was considering the picture of the good land in the Old Testament as a type of the all-inclusive Christ. There is a suggestion of this in 1:12, where Paul says that Christ is the portion of the saints. Then in 2:6 Paul tells us to walk in Christ. This implies that Christ is the land, the territory, the realm, in which we may walk. Furthermore, his reference to being rooted in Christ in 2:7 also indicates that he was thinking of the good land. In order to be rooted in Christ, He must be our land, our soil. All these are indications that the Christ revealed in Colossians is our good land.

Paul had a strong background in the Old Testament. As he was writing such Epistles as Romans, 1 Corinthians, Galatians, Colossians, and Hebrews, he must have had the Old Testament Scriptures very much in mind, and he wrote many things according to them. In particular, as Paul was writing the book of Colossians, he had before him the picture of the land of Canaan. He was aware that God's chosen people in Old Testament times enjoyed the good land as their portion. Furthermore, he realized that the good land was everything to them. It was through the good land that they could worship God and build the temple for God's testimony and for His unique dwelling place. It was through the good land that God's purpose could be fulfilled through the children of Israel. Fully realizing what the good land meant to God's chosen people, Paul composed the Epistle to the

Colossians with the portrait of the good land in mind. Therefore, if we would experience the all-inclusive Christ as revealed in this book, we need to realize that such a Christ is typified by the land of Canaan. The Christ who is typified by the good land is the processed Triune God as the life-giving Spirit. I admit that I emphasize this point again and again. This is my commission and burden from the Lord.

If we would walk in Christ as the mystery of God, we must see that, according to Paul's concept, the Christ in whom we are to walk is the good land. Concerning this matter, we need the full assurance of understanding. Message after message could be given on the subject of Christ as the good land. This matter is inexhaustible.

The first major conference held in the United States in December, 1962, was on the all-inclusive Christ typified by the land of Canaan. Those messages have been published as *The All-Inclusive Christ.* A very good hymn on the experience of Christ as life was inspired by these messages. The last stanza of this hymn *(Hymns #499) is given below:*

Oh, what a prize! Oh, what a gain!
Christ is the goal toward which I press.
Nothing I treasure, nor aught desire,
But Christ of all-inclusiveness.
My hope, my glory, and my crown
Is Christ, the One of peerlessness.

In that conference a number of messages were given on Deuteronomy 8:7-10. Based on these verses, we considered the unsearchable riches of the land: the water, the food, and the minerals. What we shared in those messages was only an introductory word. A great deal remains to be said about the riches of Christ typified by the land of Canaan.

Students of the Word realize that the Bible is not easy to understand. When I was a young Christian, I told the Lord that I did not agree with the way He wrote the Bible. According to my opinion, He should have written it in a systematic way, covering each of the major points systematically and putting all the material together under various major headings and subdivisions. Nevertheless, we must recognize that the Lord's way is the best. In the Bible the Lord speaks about a particular subject in various places. Take justification as an example. This subject is covered in more than one book. Because our capacity is so limited, the Lord knew that He could reveal only a little at a time concerning spiritual matters such as justification. This is true all the more of the revelation of Christ as our good land.

AN ALL-INCLUSIVE TYPE OF CHRIST

On the one hand, the good land is revealed in the Old Testament. On the other hand, it is concealed there. Although this statement appears contradictory, actually it is not. Because Deuteronomy describes the good land, we may say that the good land is revealed in the Old Testament. But because the meaning and significance of the good land are concealed, we may also say that the land is concealed in the Scriptures. As the Lord's children, supplied by His mercy and grace, delved into the Word, they began to realize that the good land promised by God to His chosen people is a type of Christ. If the Passover enjoyed in Egypt and the manna experienced in the wilderness were types of Christ, then the good land must also be a type of Christ.

In Joshua 5:11 and 12 we see a hint that the good land typifies Christ as the continuation of the manna. Verse 11 says that the children of Israel ate of the produce of the land. Verse 12 is especially clear: "And the manna ceased on the morrow after they had eaten of the produce of the land; neither had the children of Israel manna any more; but they did eat of the fruit of the land of Canaan that year" (Heb.). Manna was a type of Christ as the life supply for God's people. As these verses in Joshua point out, the produce of the good land is the continuation of the manna. Therefore, if the manna typified Christ, the produce of the good land must also typify Him. By means of the supply of manna in the wilderness, God's people were able to build the tabernacle as God's dwelling place. In the same principle, through the supply of the rich produce of the land they were able to build the temple as a more solid dwelling place for God. No doubt, the good land enjoyed by the children of Israel is a significant type of Christ, for through the enjoyment of it the temple was built. We may even say that it is the ultimate type of Christ found in the Scriptures. It is a complete and all-inclusive type of Christ.

To have our hearts comforted and knit together in love unto the full knowledge of Christ as the mystery of God includes having the full knowledge of Christ as typified by the good land. We need to know in detail how Christ is typified by all the items mentioned in Deuteronomy 8:7-11. He is the water that springs from valleys and hills. He is the wheat and the barley, which signify respectively the incarnated and crucified Christ and the resurrected Christ. We must go on to see how Christ is typified by the wine, oil, figs, pomegranates, and minerals. Without these verses in Deuteronomy 8, we would be short in our understanding of the all-inclusiveness of Christ.

The land is the crucial focus of the Old Testament. This is the reason that in the Old Testament the Lord speaks of the land again and again. He called out Abraham and told him that He would bring him into a certain land, which was the land of Canaan. Consider how many times from Genesis 12 to the end of the Old Testament the Lord referred to the land. Actually, the center of the Old Testament is the temple within the city built in the good land. If we know the Scriptures and have light from God, we shall realize that the center of God's eternal plan, speaking according to the type, is the land with its temple and city. Beginning with the book of Genesis, the Old Testament takes the land as the center and mentions again and again something related to the land. As we have pointed out repeatedly, the land is the figure of the all-inclusive Christ, a type of Christ as everything to us.

THE BATTLE FOR THE LAND

Satan, the enemy of God, has been doing his utmost continually to frustrate the people of God from enjoying the good land. He will do whatever he can to spoil the enjoyment of Christ as the land. Not long after God created the heavens and the earth, with the intention of giving the earth to mankind as an enjoyment, Satan did something to frustrate Him. Because of Satan's rebellion, God had to judge the universe, and due to that judgment the earth was buried beneath the waters of the deep. After a period of time, God came in to work and to recover the land from the waters of the deep. Upon this recovered land, an abundance of life came into being, and there came forth a life with the image of God, a life committed with the authority of God. However, not long afterward the enemy of God came in again to deceive man and to put God in a position where judgment upon the earth was again imperative. At the time of Noah, the recovered earth was once more put under the waters of the deep. Speaking according to the type, man was separated from the enjoyment of Christ as signified by the land. But through the redemption of the ark, Noah and his family obtained the right to possess the land and enjoy all its riches. The flood separated the people from the earth, but the ark brought Noah and his family back to the enjoyment of the earth. Once again man took possession of the land and enjoyed its riches.

However, it was not too long before the enemy did something further to spoil the enjoyment of the earth, this time through the rebellion at Babel. Therefore, out of the fallen race made rebellious by Satan, God called one man, Abraham, and told him that He would bring him into a certain land. However, even this chosen one gradually drifted away from the land into Egypt, and the Lord had to bring him back to the land. Eventually, his descendants left this land and went down into Egypt. After a long period of time, the Lord brought His people out of Egypt and back to the good land. Centuries later, the enemy moved again and sent the army from Babylon to spoil the land and capture the people. But after seventy years the Lord brought them back once more to the good land. By all this we see that the history of the Old Testament is related to the land. God's work is always to recover the land, whereas the enemy's work is always to frustrate, spoil, and hinder the enjoyment of the land and do something to bring the land into chaos. The enemy's intention is to assault the land and take it over. But after the enemy makes his attempt, God moves to fight for His people and to recover the land again.

WALKING IN THE ALL-INCLUSIVE SPIRIT

We need to be deeply impressed that this good land typifies the all-inclusive Christ. We have pointed out that in Colossians 2:7 Paul says that we have been rooted in Christ. If we have been rooted in Christ, then He must be our soil, our earth. Have you ever realized that Christ is the very land in which you are rooted, that you are a plant rooted in Christ as the soil? I deeply feel that most of the Lord's children are still in Egypt. They have experienced the Lord only as the Passover lamb. Others have come out of Egypt and enjoy Christ as their daily manna as they wander in the wilderness. But very few believers experience Christ as the realm, the sphere, in which they walk. May the Lord open our eyes to see that Christ is our good land and that we must daily walk in Him!

In Galatians 3:14 Paul says, "That the blessing of Abraham might come to the nations in Jesus Christ, that we might receive the promise of the Spirit through faith." Here Paul refers to the blessing of Abraham and the promise of the Spirit. This blessing refers to the good land, and the fulfillment of this blessing for us today is Christ as the all-inclusive Spirit. Therefore, according to Paul's concept, to walk in Christ as the good land is to walk in the all-inclusive Spirit.

In Colossians 2:6 Paul tells us to walk in Christ, but in Galatians 5:16 He charges us to walk by the Spirit. Furthermore, in Romans 8:4 he speaks of walking according to spirit. These verses indicate that the good land for us today is the all-inclusive Spirit who indwells our spirit. This all-inclusive Spirit is the all-inclusive Christ as the processed Triune God. After being processed, the Triune God is the all-inclusive Christ as the all-inclusive Spirit for us to experience. Today this all-inclusive Spirit indwells our spirit to be our good land.

A number of books written by Paul, including Romans, 1 and 2 Corinthians, Galatians, and Philippians, indicate that Christ today is the all-inclusive Spirit. Christ is the embodiment of God and the expression of God. Through incarnation, He became the last Adam, who was crucified on the cross for our redemption. In resurrection this last Adam became a life-giving Spirit (1 Cor. 15:45). Therefore, in 2 Corinthians 3:17 Paul says, "Now the Lord is that Spirit." Because Christ as the life-giving Spirit dwells in our spirit, we are one spirit with Him. In 2 Timothy 4:22 Paul says, "The Lord be with thy spirit," and in 1 Corinthians 6:17, "He that is joined unto the Lord is one spirit." Therefore, Christ as the all-inclusive good land is now in our spirit. Concerning this, we all need the riches of the full assurance of understanding.

Having the full assurance that the all-inclusive Spirit is mingled with our spirit, we should set our minds on this mingled spirit (Rom. 8:6). By doing this, we are spontaneously setting our minds on Christ. Then we must go on to walk in this mingled spirit. This means that we must live, move, behave, and have our being according to the spirit. In this way we shall experience Christ and enjoy Him as the good land. Nothing in the New Testament is more central, crucial, and vital than walking according to the mingled spirit. Christ as the all-inclusive Spirit dwells in our spirit to be our life, our person, and our everything. Our need today is to return to Him, to set our minds on the spirit, and to walk according to the spirit. This is to walk in Christ as the mystery of God.

LIFE-STUDY OF COLOSSIANS

MESSAGE TWENTY-ONE

NOT TO BE DELUDED AND CARRIED OFF FROM CHRIST

Scripture Reading: Col. 2:4, 8

According to typology, the children of Israel enjoyed Christ in three stages: in Egypt, in the wilderness, and in the good land. The Passover enjoyed in Egypt was not only for their redemption; it also strengthened them to make their exodus from Egypt. In the wilderness God's people were sustained by manna, which enabled them to build God's tabernacle and to carry it as a testimony. After the children of Israel entered into the good land, they began to enjoy the rich produce of the land. This produce made it possible for them to build the temple for a more solid testimony, Speaking according to the type, the temple in the good land is the focus of God's purpose on earth. God desires to have a dwelling place among His chosen people for His expression. God's purpose is fulfilled neither by the enjoyment of Christ as the Passover lamb in Egypt nor by the enjoyment of Christ as manna in the wilderness. His purpose is fulfilled only when His people enjoy Christ as their good land.

In 1 Corinthians we see that Paul dealt with the Corinthians according to the first two stages of the enjoyment of Christ, but not according to the third stage. In 1 Corinthians 5:7 he says, "For even Christ our passover is sacrificed for us." In the following verse he charges us to "keep the feast." These verses point to the enjoyment of Christ as the Passover in Egypt. In 1 Corinthians 10:3 and 4 Paul refers to spiritual food and spiritual drink. This refers to the enjoyment of Christ in the wilderness. In 1 Corinthians there is no mention of the third stage of the enjoyment of Christ. But in Colossians Paul regarded the believers as being in this stage of the enjoyment of Christ.

Because the Corinthians were not in the third stage of the enjoyment of Christ, the church life in that locality was a tabernacle church life, a church life that was portable and that lacked a solid foundation. By contrast, the church life in Ephesians, Colossians, and Philippians is that of the temple. It is a settled church life with a solid foundation. Stone was not used in the building of the tabernacle, but a great deal of stone was used in constructing the temple. For this reason, the temple, the enlargement of the tabernacle, was solid and settled.

The church life in Colossians and Ephesians is more solid than that in 1 Corinthians because in these Epistles the enjoyment of Christ is not elementary. It is not merely the enjoyment of Christ as the Passover or as the manna, but the enjoyment of Christ as the good land, as the portion of the saints. Today some churches may be in the first or second stage of the enjoyment of Christ, whereas others may be in the third stage.

If we would enter into the good land, we must conquer and subdue all the enemies typified by the seven tribes. These enemies are the evil rulers, authorities, principalities, and powers in the air. After these enemies have been defeated, we shall have peace, and in this peace the temple can be built.

I. NOT TO BE DELUDED

A. By Judaizers or by Gnostics

Although the Colossians were in Christ as the good land, they had been deluded, deceived. This was the reason that Paul said in 2:4, "This I say that no one may delude you with persuasive speech."

In order for believers to be deluded, something close to the truth must be used to deceive them. For example, counterfeit money or forged checks are deceptive because their appearance is close to that of the real things. People would never be deceived by money or by checks that are obviously false. In like manner, the Colossians were deceived by observances and practices that were close to the experience of Christ. Furthermore, certain aspects of Gnosticism were similar to the teachings of the Bible. For this reason, the Colossians could be deceived.

It is very easy to be deceived by something that is close to the real thing, by a counterfeit that is almost identical to something genuine. Without the proper discernment, it is difficult to see the difference between the teachings in the New Testament and ethical teachings like those of Confucius. When I was young, I heard a missionary say that the ethical teachings of Confucius were the same as some teachings in the Bible. The Bible teaches that wives should submit to their husbands. Confucius, however, teaches a threefold submission. Firstly, a woman is to submit to her father; then to her husband; and then, should her husband die, to her son. Concerning submission, the teachings of Confucius and the teachings of the Bible appear to be the same in principle. If we do not have discernment, we could be led astray from Christ by ethical teachings that appear to be the same as those of the Bible.

Many aspects of the Jewish religion are very good. Take, for example, the dietary regulations in Leviticus 11 and the commandment to keep the Sabbath. It seems right that, just as God rested on the seventh day after laboring for six days, man should have a day of rest after six days of labor. However, there is a problem here. According to the Bible, should we labor first and then rest, or should we rest first and then labor? We may think that because God rested after working for six days, we should do the same. But if we have light from God, we shall see that in the Scriptures God first labors and then rests, but man first rests and then works. Man was created on the sixth day, toward the end of the six days of God's labor. After the creation of man, God rested, and man rested with God. This indicates that as soon as man came into being, he had a time of rest. Therefore, according to the principle in the Bible, we are to rest before we work. In the New Testament we see that first we receive grace, and then we work. To work before receiving grace is to live according to the law. But to receive grace before we work is according to God's salvation by grace. If we are not clear about this, we may be deceived by the teaching of the Seventh-Day Adventists regarding the keeping of the Sabbath. We need to tell the Seventh-Day Adventists that with God work came before rest, but with us rest comes before work. According to the New Testament, receiving grace precedes working. If we do not receive grace as the capital, we shall have nothing with which to work. We cannot work unless we first receive grace. This is a basic principle.

These examples show that certain observances and teachings are similar to some aspects of God's salvation. This was the reason that the believers in Colosse could be deceived by Jewish observances and pagan teachings and could allow those things to pervade the church life. I am concerned that the young ones may be deluded by those who advocate certain teachings or practices. We need to have a thorough understanding of the basic principles in the New Testament. Then we shall have the wisdom and the knowledge to convince and subdue those who attempt to delude us.

Paul opens 2:4 with the words, "This I say." These words refer to what Paul has covered in verses 2 and 3 concerning the riches of the full assurance of understanding, the full knowledge of Christ as the mystery of God, and the fact that all the treasures of wisdom and knowledge are hidden in Christ. Paul emphasized these things so that the saints at Colosse would not be deluded. If we have seen the revelation of Christ in Colossians 1, we shall not be deceived by teachings concerning such things as water baptism and the observance of the Sabbath. We shall know that the all-inclusive Christ is the focus of God's economy and everything to us. If we have a clear vision of Christ, no one will be able to delude us or deceive us.

B. With Persuasive Speech

In verse 4 Paul specifically refers to "persuasive speech." Usually those who deceive others are eloquent and persuasive in speech. Beware of eloquence. A speaker may be very eloquent, but there may be no reality in his speech. Instead of being taken in by a speaker's eloquence, we should ask if there is reality in his speaking.

Sister M. E. Barber helped Brother Nee to learn this important lesson. When he was young, Brother Nee was attracted by the eloquence and knowledge of certain visiting preachers. Whenever Brother Nee expressed his admiration for a speaker's eloquence, Sister Barber would point out that although that preacher was eloquent and knowledgeable, there was no life ministered in his speaking. On one occasion in particular, Brother Nee thought that a certain preacher's message was marvelous, and he was confident that Sister Barber would agree. Nevertheless, Sister Barber still pointed out that the message was void of life and reality. From that time onward, Brother Nee no longer appreciated the empty speech of eloquent preachers. May we also learn not to be deluded by persuasive speech.

If we see the vision of the all-inclusive Christ presented in the book of Colossians, we shall not be deluded by anything. No matter how excellent or how scriptural a thing; may be, it will not be able to lead us away from Christ. It is crucial that we have such a view of Christ in God's economy.

The situation of the church at Colosse was very different from that of the church in Corinth. In Corinth, the standard was low, there were divisions, and some saints were involved in lawsuits, some even in fornication. But at Colosse the standard of behavior was much higher. As we have pointed out, the problem at Colosse was that the church had been invaded by culture, especially by Gnosticism and the Judaistic observances. These things were very refined, and for this very reason they were deceitful. Hence, we in the Lord's recovery today must be cautious of those who appear to be highly cultured and well-educated and who speak in a gentle and humble manner. Those who are the most deceitful usually seem to be very nice. No doubt, when the serpent approached Eve in the garden, he spoke in a very refined way. Be on the alert lest you are deluded through the persuasive speech of cultured people. Only when we have a clear view of the place of the all-inclusive Christ in God's economy shall we be able to see through delusion and deception.

II. NOT TO BE CARRIED OFF AS CAPTIVE

In verse 8 Paul goes on to say, "Beware that no one carries you off as spoil through his philosophy and empty deceit." The first step, seen in verse 4, is to be deluded; the second step, seen in verse 8, is to be carried off as spoil. The word spoil here does not mean to damage; it means to be a prey or a captive. Those who are carried off as spoil are carried off into captivity.

A. Through Philosophy and Empty Deceit

We need to beware that no one carries us off as spoil through his philosophy. In Greek the word rendered "his" is the emphatic article. Hence, it denotes a particular philosophy. The philosophy through which the believers at Colosse were carried off as spoil was Gnosticism, a mixture of Jewish, oriental, and Greek philosophies. As Paul indicates, Gnosticism is empty deceit. Actually, every form of deceit is empty. Nothing that is real, that has real content, can be a deceit.

B. According to the Tradition of Men

The philosophy and empty deceit in this verse is "according to the tradition of men, according to the elements of the world, and not according to Christ." The source of the Gnostic teaching at Colosse was the tradition of men. It did not depend on the revealed writings of God, but on the traditional practices of men. Many cultural traditions are good. Otherwise, no one would care for them. We need to have a keen discernment to be kept from being deceived by the traditions in Catholicism and the denominations. One principle we should follow is that of testing everything with the Bible. We should care only for God's direct revelation in the holy Word, not for anything that is according to the tradition of men. We need not accept anything inherited from men as a tradition if it does not correspond to the divine revelation in the Bible.

Today's Roman Catholics are bound by their traditions. Instead of referring to what the Bible says or to what God says, they often stand on what the church says or on what is taught by the priests and nuns. On some occasions I have pointed out to certain Catholics the error of worshipping Mary and have shown them that this is not according to the Bible. Nevertheless, they said that the worship of Mary is according to the teaching of the Catholic church. Other Catholic traditions are related to placing candles before images and praying to the saints to shorten the time that a relative must spend in purgatory. Although practices of this kind are not according to the Bible, Catholics follow them because of tradition. The traditions of men are also found in the denominations and in the independent Christian groups, where many believers care more for the tradition of men than for the Word of God.

C. According to the Elements of the World

The philosophy and empty deceit are not only according to the tradition of men, but also according to the elements of the world. Here and in 2:20 and Galatians 4:3, this expression does not refer to substances; it refers to the rudimentary teachings of both Jews and Gentiles, teachings that consist of ritualistic observances in meats, drinks, washings, and asceticism. In the eyes of Paul, the traditions of men were merely elementary principles. These traditions are included with the elementary principles of the world.

D. Not According to Christ

Paul concludes verse 8 by saying that the philosophy and empty deceit are not according to Christ. Christ is the governing principle of all genuine wisdom and knowledge, the reality of all genuine teaching, and the only measure of all concepts acceptable to God. The book of Colossians focuses on Christ as our everything.

To fall short of being according to Christ, firstly means that we do not take Christ as life (3:4). Secondly, it means that we do not hold Christ as the Head of the Body. Furthermore, it is not to know Christ as the mystery of God (2:2), nor to experience the indwelling Christ as the hope of glory (1:27). Finally, to be not according to Christ means that we do not walk in Christ (2:6).

If we take Christ as life, hold Him as the Head of the Body, know Him as the mystery of God, experience Him as the hope of glory, and walk in Him as the all-inclusive Spirit, then we shall not be deceived by anything or by anyone. Those who do not experience Christ in these aspects can easily be deceived. If you analyze the situation of those who have been deluded and carried off as spoil, you will realize that they did not experience Christ in these five ways. They did not realize that Christ alone is everything in God's economy, and they did not take Christ as their life or as their Head. Furthermore, they did not experience the indwelling Christ as their hope of glory, nor did they live, move, and have their being in Christ. As a result, they were defenseless, and eventually were deluded and carried off into captivity. Our defense against deception is the Christ who is our life, our Head, the mystery of God, the hope of glory, and the good land in which we walk.

I believe that all these messages on the all-inclusive Christ will help to guard us against delusion and against being carried off as prey. They will build up a strong defense for us in the Lord's recovery. Without such a defense, we can easily be deluded and carried off as spoil. But if we experience Christ as the center of God's economy in all these aspects, we shall be protected, and we shall not be deluded or carried off as spoil.

LIFE-STUDY OF COLOSSIANS

MESSAGE TWENTY-TWO

MADE FULL AND CIRCUMCISED IN CHRIST

Scripture Reading: Col. 2:9-12, 18, 20-22; 1 Cor. 1:30; Eph. 3:8

After warning us to beware that no one carries us off as spoil through philosophy and empty deceit, Paul tells us that in Christ dwells all the fullness of the Godhead bodily (2:9). Then in verse 10 he goes on to say, "And you in Him are made full, Who is the Head of all rule and authority." In Christ we lack nothing, for in Him we have been perfected and completed. There is no reason for us to turn to anything other than Christ. As we shall see, in speaking these words Paul was dealing with the matter of angel worship.

Then in verse 11 Paul says that we were circumcised in Christ. To be made full in Him is positive, whereas to be circumcised is to deal with something negative, in particular, the flesh, the self, and the natural man. All these things have been removed by the circumcision which is in Christ. In this message we need to consider how in Christ, on the positive side, we have been made full and, on the negative side, we have been circumcised.

I. MADE FULL IN CHRIST

A. Christ as the Embodiment of All the Fullness of the Godhead

In 2:9 Paul says, "For in Him dwells all the fullness of the Godhead bodily." This means that Christ is the embodiment of the fullness of the Godhead, that the fullness of the Triune God dwells in Christ in a bodily form. The fact that the fullness of the Godhead dwells in Christ bodily means that it dwells in Him in a way that is both real and practical.

B. Made Full in Christ

Because all the fullness of the Godhead is in Christ and because we have been placed in Him (1 Cor. 1:30), we have been made full in Him. The New Testament reveals clearly that all those who believe in Christ have been put into Christ. Therefore, we are identified with Him and one with Him. The result is that all He is and all He has belongs to us, and all that He has experienced is our history. We inherit all that Christ has experienced and passed through. Furthermore, because we are one with Him, we partake of all that He has accomplished, obtained, and attained.

Marriage is an illustration of this. Suppose a poor woman marries a very rich man. Because she is joined to her husband and identified with him, she partakes of all that he is and has. Likewise, we are members of the all-inclusive Christ. We have been put into Him, identified with Him, truly "married" to Him. Hence, we are one with Him. All that He has passed through is now our history, and all that He has obtained and attained is our inheritance. We are in such a Christ, and He is in us. We have been placed into Him, we are one with Him, and we receive all that He is and has.

Although some Christians have a doctrinal knowledge of this, a mere mental understanding of our union with Christ is not adequate. We need to exercise faith in order to partake of all that is ours in Christ. We should not consider ourselves poor, just as a poor woman who has married a rich man should no longer think of herself as poor. Even though she may feel poor, she must practice applying the fact that the riches of her husband belong to her. In like manner, because we are one with Christ, we should not regard ourselves as in poverty. To the contrary, we need to have a full realization of what we have in Christ.

In their prayers, some Christians like to declare how poor, pitiful, and low they are. This kind of prayer is without faith or assurance. We need to believe with full assurance that we are one with the rich, all-inclusive Christ, with the

One who is the embodiment of all the fullness of the Triune God. If we realize this with full assurance, we shall never consider ourselves poor.

Do not believe your feelings about yourself, but look away to Christ. Exercise your faith to realize what He is, what He has passed through, what He has obtained and attained, and where He is today. Since He is in the third heaven and we are one with Him, we are in the third heaven also. In Christ we are not only millionaires—we are billionaires. We have been placed into the Christ who is unsearchably rich.

In this Christ we are made perfect, complete. In Him we do not lack anything. Do not talk about how much you lack. Because you are in Christ, you lack nothing. In Him is the fullness, the perfection, the completion. Actually, He Himself is the fullness, perfection, and completion. Because we are in Him, we are complete and perfect; we lack nothing. We are those who possess the riches of Christ.

In Ephesians 3:8 Paul speaks of the unsearchable riches of Christ. We are more than billionaires because the riches we have are greater than can be counted. We simply have no idea what vast riches we possess in Christ. Often we have prayed, "Lord, I am poor and pitiful." But not many have prayed in this way: "Lord, I thank You that I am rich, complete, and full. Lord Jesus, because I am in You, I am richer than the wealthiest billionaire. I am short of nothing." I hope that after reading this message, you will begin to pray in this way. Tell the Lord, the angels, and even the demons that you are richer than any earthly billionaire because you are in the Christ whose riches are unsearchable.

C. Christ as the Head of All Rule and Authority

In 2:10 Paul says that Christ is the Head of all rule and authority. The rule and authority spoken of here are the angelic powers, in particular the fallen angels who still occupy positions of power. According to the full revelation of the Bible, after God created the universe, He placed it under the control of an archangel and other leading angels. When this archangel rebelled against God and became Satan, many of the leading angels who assisted him in ruling the universe became the evil rulers and authorities in the heavenlies. These are described in Ephesians 6:12 as the rulers, the authorities, the world-rulers of this darkness, the spiritual forces of evil in the heavenlies. These angelic powers rule over the nations. For this reason, in the book of Daniel there is mention both of the prince of Greece and of the prince of Persia. (A prince here denotes one of the angelic powers or rulers.) This means that all the nations on earth today are under the rule of authorities in the heavenlies; however, not all of these are evil. But Christ is the Head of all rule and authority.

Since Christ is our perfection and completion, we do not need other rules and authorities as objects of adoration, for He is the Head of all these. Remember that the Colossians had been led astray to the worship of angels. Therefore, Paul told them that since Christ is the Head of all the angels and since we are in Him, there is no need for us to worship angels.

The Colossians were worshipping angels because they fell under the influence of the heretical teaching that God is too exalted to be worshipped directly by lowly human beings. According to this false doctrine, we must humble ourselves and worship the angels as mediators between us and God. Those who worship angels in this way argue that they are still worshipping God, not idols. They claim simply to be worshipping God through the mediation of angels, who are superior to us. This heresy became prevailing in Asia Minor. Therefore, Paul was burdened to point out their error. How wrong the Colossians were in taking the angels as mediators! There is one mediator between God and men, the man Christ Jesus (1 Tim. 2:5). Since the Colossians were in the very One who is the Head of all angels and since they had been made full in Him, they were not short of anything. They had no need of angels to be mediators. Angels are to serve us and to protect us, but they are not mediators between us and God. All the saints have at least one angel, one angelic bodyguard, assigned to serve them and protect them. This is proved by the

Lord's word in Matthew 18:10 where He charges us not to despise "one of these little ones, for...their angels in the heavens always behold the face of My Father Who is in the heavens." Furthermore, when Peter was released from prison and was knocking at the door of the gate, those inside the house told the young woman, who kept saying that Peter was knocking, "It is his angel" (Acts 12:15). Although the angels serve us and may protect us, we should not regard them as mediators. Because they are servants, we should not worship them. We are identified with the One who is the Head of all the angels, and in Him we have been made full. If we are clear about this, we shall never be deluded into worshipping angels. Rather, we shall have the proper knowledge that, in a very real sense, because we are one with the Head of the angels, we are higher than they are. Actually, we are partners of the Christ who is the Head over them, and in Him we are complete.

This fact of having been made full in Christ is versus the worship of angels. Because we are one with Christ, we should never worship angels.

II. CIRCUMCISED IN CHRIST

A. With a Circumcision Not Made with Hands

In verse 11 Paul says, "In Whom also you were circumcised with a circumcision not made with hands, in the putting off of the body of the flesh, in the circumcision of Christ." Here Paul speaks of a circumcision not made with hands. This certainly is different from that practiced by the Jews, which was carried out with a knife. In addition to that physical circumcision, there is another kind of circumcision, the circumcision in Christ, which is not made with hands. This is spiritual circumcision and refers to the proper baptism, which puts off the body of the flesh by the effectual virtue of the death of Christ. As we shall see, this is versus asceticism.

The circumcision in Christ involves the death of Christ and the power of the Spirit. When Christ was crucified on the cross, His crucifixion was the genuine, practical, and universal circumcision. His crucifixion cut off all the negative things. These negative things include our flesh, our natural man, and the self. However, along with the death of Christ we need the Spirit as the power. If we have Christ's crucifixion without the Spirit as the power, we shall have no means to apply Christ's crucifixion to us and to execute its effect upon us. The crucifixion of Christ becomes practical and effective by means of the Spirit. By the Spirit as the power, Christ's crucifixion is applied to us. Then under the power of the Spirit, we are circumcised in an actual and practical way. This is the circumcision in Christ, a circumcision not made with hands. It is a circumcision not made with hands because it was accomplished by the death of Christ, and it is applied, executed, and carried out by the powerful Spirit. This is the circumcision we have all received.

In Christ, on the one hand, we have been made full, and, on the other hand, we have been circumcised. Because we have been made full in Him, we are short of nothing. Because we have been circumcised in Him, all the negative things have been removed. Regarding the positive things, we are complete. Regarding the negative things, everything has been cleared up, and we have no problems. Therefore, regarding the positive things, we are not short of anything, and regarding the negative things, we are no longer troubled by anything.

However, we need to exercise faith and not look at ourselves. We must turn our eyes away from our feelings and from our apparent situation. According to our apparent situation, we are short of everything positive and are troubled by everything negative. But according to the facts, we are not in ourselves—we are in Christ. Because we are in Him, we have been made full positively, and we have been circumcised to clear away the negative things.

B. In the Putting Off of the Body of the Flesh

In verse 11 Paul speaks of "the putting off of the body of the flesh." This means to strip off something, as to strip off clothing. The circumcision that took place by the death of

Christ and is applied by the powerful Spirit accomplishes the putting off of the body of the flesh. Our body of flesh was crucified on the cross with Christ and has been put off. Regarding this, we must again exercise our faith and not consider our self and our apparent situation. Let us exercise faith and say, "Amen! The body of the flesh has been put off on the cross and by the powerful Spirit."

C. In the Circumcision of Christ

This circumcision must be in the circumcision of Christ, not with a circumcision made with hands. The circumcision of Christ is by His crucifixion. Our flesh has been crossed out by His death on the cross.

D. Through Baptism

Furthermore, the circumcision in Christ takes place through baptism. In verse 12 Paul says, "Buried together with Him in baptism, in Whom also you were raised together through the faith of the operation of God, Who raised Him from among the dead." We have been buried together with Christ in baptism. To be buried in baptism is to put off the body of the flesh, to disrobe or strip it off. Moreover, in Christ we have been raised together through the faith of the operation of God. In baptism there is the burial aspect, which is the termination of our flesh, and the raising aspect, which is the germination of our spirit. In the raising aspect we are made alive in Christ with the divine life.

In this verse Paul points out that this is through the faith of the operation of God. Faith is not of ourselves; it is the gift of God (Eph. 2:8). The more we turn to God and contact Him, the more faith we have. The Lord is the Author and Perfecter of our faith (Heb. 12:2). The more we abide in Him, the more we are infused with Him as our faith. It is through this living faith in the operation of the living God that we experience the resurrection life, signified by the raising aspect of baptism. Many Christians today neglect the real operation of baptism. Instead, they pay attention to the kind of water used or to the method of placing people under the water.

Genuine baptism involves an operation in which we are buried and terminated. This operation involves the exercise of faith. The One who carries out the operation is the Spirit. Whenever we baptize someone, there is the need for the exercise of faith to realize that an operation is taking place to terminate the old being of the one who is to be baptized. We must have faith in the operation of God, the Triune God, who raised Christ from among the dead.

Whenever we baptize a new believer, we must realize that this one is being placed into a divine operation that will terminate him and bury him. We must exercise faith in the operation of the Triune God. By faith we have the reality of the termination and burial of the old man, the self, the flesh, and the natural life. The operating Triune God will honor this faith by making these things real. This burial and termination of the old man through baptism is the real circumcision.

E. Circumcision versus Asceticism

Since the Colossians had received such a circumcision, there was no need for them to practice asceticism. Being circumcised in the circumcision of Christ is versus asceticism (2:20-22). Those who have been buried and terminated and who are now resting in the tomb, have no need of asceticism. There is no reason for them to treat their bodies severely. This is against the spiritual principle. According to the spiritual principle, we have been terminated and have put off the body of the flesh, the very thing that asceticism attempts to deal with. Every form of asceticism attempts to deal with the lusts of the flesh. According to the teaching and practice of asceticism, treating the body severely eliminates lusts and restricts indulgence. This is the basic principle of asceticism. In India some practice asceticism by sitting on a bed of needles. Whenever they become conscious of fleshly lusts, they press against the needles, thinking that the pain they inflict on themselves will restrict their lusts. This same principle explains ascetic rules about eating delicious foods. According to asceticism, to enjoy food is to indulge the flesh. For this reason, ascetics are taught to choose food that is not palatable.

As we shall point out in a later message, this severe treatment of the body is "not of any value against the indulgence of the flesh" (2:23). The various practices of asceticism are not effective in restricting the indulgence of the flesh. Paul's concept in Colossians 2 was that since the believers in Christ had been circumcised in the circumcision of Christ, which was accomplished by Christ's death and is applied by the Spirit, and since this is the circumcision in which they have been buried and terminated, there is absolutely no need for the practice of asceticism. To mistreat the body in the attempt to restrict the indulgence of the flesh is foolish and of no avail. Truly the circumcision in Christ is versus asceticism.

In this message we have seen that, positively, we have been made full in Christ and that, negatively, we have been circumcised in Him. Therefore, there is no need for us to worship angels or to practice asceticism. Although these practices were prevailing among the Colossians, we should utterly cast them aside. We do not worship angels, and we do not practice asceticism. We are in Christ. In Him we have been made full and are short of nothing. In Him we have been circumcised from every negative thing. For this reason, we do not need asceticism to restrict the indulgence of the flesh. This was the concept of the Apostle Paul. I believe that his writing concerning this matter in Colossians 2 will be helpful to us today.

LIFE-STUDY OF COLOSSIANS

MESSAGE TWENTY-THREE

THE ECONOMY OF GOD'S SALVATION

Scripture Reading: Col. 2:13-15, 18, 20-22; Eph. 2:5, 15

In this message we shall consider the economy of God's salvation as it is revealed in 2:13-15. As we shall see, this economy involves three things: making us alive with Christ, abolishing the ritual law, and stripping off the evil angelic powers.

THE THREE ASPECTS

Colossians 2:13 says, "And you, being dead in the offenses and in the uncircumcision of your flesh, He made alive together with Him, having forgiven us all offenses." The word dead here refers to the deadness in spirit because of sin. We who once were dead in offenses and in the uncircumcision of the flesh have been made alive together with Christ. This means that God has enlivened us in Christ's resurrection with the divine life. What was accomplished in Christ's resurrection (1 Pet. 1:3) is experienced through our faith. The first aspect in the economy of God's salvation is that He has made us alive together with the resurrected Christ.

In verse 14 Paul goes on to say, "Wiping out the handwriting in ordinances which was against us, which was contrary to us; and He has taken it out of the way, nailing it to the cross." The Greek word rendered "wiping out" can also be translated blotting out, obliterating, erasing, or annulling (a decree of law). The Greek word rendered "handwriting" denotes a legal document, a bond. Here it refers to the written law. The ordinances, or decrees, refer to the ceremonial law with its rituals, the forms or ways of living and worship. These ordinances God has taken out of the way by nailing them to the cross. This is to abolish the law of the commandments in ordinances (Eph. 2:15). This kills the heresy of keeping the Judaistic rituals.

In verse 15 Paul continues, "Stripping off the rulers and the authorities, He made a display of them openly, triumphing over them in it." The Greek for "stripping off" can also be rendered "putting off," as in 3:9. The rulers and authorities spoken of in this verse are the angelic rulers and authorities. Because of the heretical teaching of angel-worship at Colosse, the passage here refers to the evil angels. The law was given through angels (Acts 7:53; Gal. 3:19). Based upon this, the heretical teachers at Colosse advocated the worship of angels (Col. 2:18) as mediators between God and man. Hence, the apostle dealt with this heresy by unveiling the fact that the law, consisting of ordinances, was nailed to the cross (v. 14), and the leading evil angels were stripped off from God. This left Christ as the sole Mediator, who is the Head of all rule and authority (v. 10). This kills the heresy of angel worship.

In verses 13, 14, and 15 the pronoun He refers to God in verse 12. The Greek word for make a display means show or exhibit in the sense of putting to an open shame. God openly shamed the evil angelic rulers and authorities on the cross and triumphed over them in it. The Greek words translated "in it" refer to the cross, but they can also be rendered in Him, referring to Christ.

It is not God's intention that we keep the law, and He certainly does not want us to worship angels. God's desire is to enliven human beings who are dead in offenses. In order to enliven us, He must put His very life into us. When His life comes into us, we are enlivened, made alive.

NO PLACE FOR THE LAW OR THE ANGELS

By mentioning the enlivening of those who are dead in offenses together with the ordinances of the law and the angels, Paul's intention is to point out that the concept held by the Colossians was altogether wrong. The Colossians still regarded the law and the angels very highly. They placed a high value on the ordinances of the law, and they were even worshipping certain of the angels. Although God has used both the law and the angels, in the economy of His salvation there is no place either for the law or for the angels. Angels are not admitted into the sphere of God's salvation. Every believer has an angel, but these angels do not share in God's salvation. Christ's redemption has nothing to do with angels. In the realm of God's economy in His salvation, both the law and the angels are ruled out. In the eyes of God, the ordinances, rituals, and ceremonies of the law have been crucified on the cross. However, not many Christians realize this. Not only were sin, the natural man, the world, and Satan crucified on the cross; the law was also crucified there. For this reason, in 2:14 Paul says that God wiped out the handwriting in ordinances by nailing it to the cross. Because Paul's vision was so clear, his word was very definite. As evil men were putting Christ on the cross, God was nailing the law to the cross. Although the law had been given by God through angels, God Himself nailed it to the cross of Christ.

Verse 14 is a powerful weapon to counteract the teaching of the Seventh-Day Adventists about the observance of the Sabbath. Observing the Sabbath is one of the ordinances, or rituals, of the law that has been nailed to the cross. According to 2:14, the ordinances have been taken out of the way and nailed to the cross. Hence, the Seventh-Day Adventists need to see that the Sabbath-keeping ordinances have been wiped out. The very thing they treasure God has taken away. Actually, the ordinance of keeping the Sabbath was against us and contrary to us. Because God loves us, He has taken away this ordinance for our sake. Nevertheless, the Seventh-Day Adventists seek to restore the very thing God has removed.

Do not argue with Seventh-Day Adventists about which day, the seventh or the eighth, should be observed. Rather, point out that the keeping of the Sabbath is part of the handwriting in ordinances which has been taken away. We may use 2:14 boldly as a weapon to annihilate the ordinance concerning observing the Sabbath. In God's economy of His salvation, there is no room for the law. Just as sin has been crucified on the cross, so the law has been crucified also. Both have been nailed to the cross of Christ. God does not want either sin or the law to remain. What He desires is for us to exist together with the risen Christ.

STRIPPING OFF THE RULERS AND AUTHORITIES

We have pointed out that at the time of Christ's crucifixion God stripped off, put off, the rulers and authorities. When Christ was crucified, the leading evil angels attempted to surround God when Christ was on the cross. But God used the cross to strip off these angels. This is Paul's concept in these verses.

In a very real sense, the cross of Christ is the center of the universe. After God created the heavens, the earth, and the billions of items in the universe, an archangel rebelled, and many angels followed him. This archangel became Satan, and his followers became the evil rulers, powers, and authorities in the heavenlies. Eventually, the man created by God fell and became sinful. The rebellion of the angels and the fall of man put God into a difficult situation. God's way to deal with this difficulty is the cross. Firstly, God became a man, thereby putting humanity on Himself. Then Christ, God incarnate, went to the cross and was crucified. During the thirty-three and a half years of His earthly life, Christ walked from the manger to the cross. When He was crucified, many things took place. On the cross God judged sin and the sinful old man. Through the cross, our sinful nature was terminated. At the very time God was judging sin and sinful man, He also nailed the law to the cross. When God was nailing the law to the cross, the evil angels also were present and very active. But, according to verse 15, God stripped them off through the cross.

We have pointed out that, according to 2:15, God stripped off the rulers and authorities. From what or from where did He strip them off? If we would answer this question, we must see that while Christ was on the cross, God was working. At that time, the cross was the center of the universe.

The Savior, sin, Satan, we, and God all were there. God was there judging sin and nailing the law to the cross. As He was doing this, the rulers and authorities gathered around God and Christ. We have pointed out that, according to grammar, the subject of verses 13 through 15 is God. Thus, the He in verse 15 denotes God. God made us alive together with Christ, nailed the ordinances to the cross, stripped off the rulers and authorities, made a display of them openly, and triumphed over them. No doubt, the rulers and authorities had swarmed around Christ as He was being crucified. Both God and Christ were working. Christ's work was His crucifixion, whereas God's work was to judge sin and all the negative things and to nail the law with its ordinances to the cross. The rulers and authorities who had gathered around God and Christ were also working. If they had not pressed in closely, how could God have stripped them off? The words "stripping off" indicate that they were very close, as close as our garments are to our body. By stripping off the rulers and authorities, God made a display of them openly. He openly put them to shame and triumphed over them. What a great matter this is!

WAR AT THE CROSS

Colossians 2:15 portrays the fighting that took place at the time of Christ's crucifixion. Evil men had put Christ on the cross. By His crucifixion Christ labored to accomplish redemption. God the Father was also working to judge sin and to nail the law to the cross. At the same time, the rulers and authorities were busy in the attempt to frustrate the work of God and Christ. The reference to triumph in verse 15 implies fighting. It indicates that a war was raging. While Christ was accomplishing redemption and God was dealing with the law and with the negative things, the rulers and authorities came to interfere. They pressed in close to God and Christ. But at that very juncture, God stripped them off, triumphed over them, and made a display of them openly, putting them to an open shame.

Colossians 2:15 is a small window through which we behold a marvelous sight. At the time of Christ's crucifixion, a battle was raging between God and the rulers and authorities. But God stripped them off and triumphed over them.

PAUL'S CONCEPT

Paul's concept in these verses is that the law and the angels have been set aside through the cross. The law was nailed to the cross, and the evil angels have been stripped off by means of the cross. Therefore, in God's economy in His salvation there is room neither for the law nor for the angelic rulers. How wrong the Colossians were in following ordinances and in worshipping angels! The law with its ordinances, including the keeping of the Sabbath, had been nailed to the cross. The Colossians were altogether wrong in allowing these things to pervade the church. Furthermore, in the cross God overcame the angelic rulers and put them to shame. What a blunder to be led astray to worship angels!

A PEACEFUL ENVIRONMENT FOR THE ENLIVENING OF HIS CHOSEN ONES

If we see the vision conveyed in these verses, many problems will be solved. For example, no one will be able to convince us to go back to the observance of the seventh day Sabbath. No one will be able to persuade us to be subject to the ordinances God has nailed to the cross. To follow such ordinances is to be blind and in darkness. It is to be ignorant of the Bible or to know it only superficially. Those who advocate Sabbath keeping may appeal to certain verses in the Old Testament. They may try to argue that both the Lord Jesus and Paul went to the synagogue on the Sabbath. However, 2:14 and 16 make it clear that the ordinances, including the observance of the Sabbath, have been abolished. Those who advocate the observance of the Sabbath have never touched the depths of the Scripture. They do not realize that through the cross the ordinances have been abolished. Furthermore, the rulers and authorities who gathered around God and Christ in displeasure at what was taking place on the cross have been defeated. When these evil angels surrounded God and Christ, God overcame them and stripped them off. Therefore, the law has been nailed to the cross, and the rulers and the authorities have been stripped off from God. What remains now is God's redeemed people who are in a position to be enlivened by Him. Now that the law and the angels have been set aside, God has a clear ground and a peaceful environment for the enlivening of His chosen ones. He now has a proper atmosphere to carry out the pleasant task of enlivening the very ones He chose in eternity past. He delights to put His life into them and to make them alive.

The Colossians needed to see such a vision, and we also need to see it today. Because they lacked this vision, the Colossians were trying to keep the law and were worshipping angels. How foolish!

The aspects of the economy of God's salvation in 2:13-15 are presented in a good sequence. In the economy of His salvation God enlivens us, nails the law to the cross, and strips off the evil rulers and authorities. The law is a frustration, and the rulers and authorities are troublesome. Because God has removed the law and the angels, we, His chosen people, are alone with Him. We are no longer bothered by terms, conditions, or requirements. God is here to enliven us, and we are here to be enlivened by Him. We should forget the law and the angels and allow God to put Himself into us as life.

The law that was used to expose our sinfulness has been nailed to the cross. Furthermore, the angels have been stripped off from God and Christ. Have you ever realized that at the time of the crucifixion God and Christ were so busy? Have you ever seen that the evil rulers and authorities were swarming around God and Christ and that a warfare was raging at the cross? I believe that few Christians have seen these things. Praise the Lord that by triumphing over the angelic powers and stripping them off, God has cleared the ground to enliven His chosen people.

Because of the subtlety of the enemy, the believers at Colosse were returning to the ordinances of the law and even were worshipping angels. What a great heresy! The principle is the same among Christians today. Christians may follow various ordinances, and those in Catholicism may even worship angels. Those who do not worship angels may still greatly admire them and unconsciously aspire to be like angels. Many sisters especially desire a type of angelic spirituality. But in principle to admire angels is to adore them, to worship them. I can testify that in me there is no place for angels. God has the ground to contact me in Christ. The law and the angels are not between me and Him.

The environment and the atmosphere are very suitable for God to contact us. Furthermore, God is not here to judge us, for He has already judged us on the cross. He is not even here to deal with us, because He has dealt with us already. God is here to accomplish one thing—to enliven us by imparting life into us. As the life-giving Spirit, the Triune God is giving life to us. In the meetings of the church life, we are being enlivened. Concerning this, the law and the angels have no place. We should remind the rulers and authorities that at Calvary God stripped them off and triumphed over them. Based upon God's victory, we can order them to flee. What we need today is not the law or the angels, but the enlivening One, the life-giving One. This is the economy of God's salvation.

About the Author

Witness Lee was born in 1905 in northern China and raised in a Christian family. At age 19 he was fully captured for Christ and immediately consecrated himself to preach the gospel for the rest of his life. Early in his service, he met Watchman Nee, a renowned preacher, teacher, and writer. Witness Lee labored together with Watchman Nee under his direction. In 1934 Watchman Nee entrusted Witness Lee with the responsibility for his publication operation, called the Shanghai Gospel Bookroom.

Prior to the Communist takeover in 1949, Witness Lee was sent by Watchman Nee and his other co-workers to Taiwan to ensure that the things delivered to them by the Lord would not be lost. Watchman Nee instructed Witness Lee to continue the former's publishing operation abroad as the Taiwan Gospel Bookroom, which has been publicly recognized as the publisher of Watchman Nee's works outside China. Witness Lee's work in Taiwan manifested the Lord's abundant blessing. From a mere 350 believers, newly fled from the mainland, the churches in Taiwan grew to 20,000 in five years.

In 1962 Witness Lee felt led of the Lord to come to the United States, settling in California. During his 35 years of service in the U.S., he ministered in weekly meetings and weekend conferences, delivering several thousand spoken messages. Much of his speaking has since been published as over 400 titles. Many of these have been translated into over fourteen languages. He gave his last public conference in February 1997 at the age of 91.

He leaves behind a prolific presentation of the truth in the Bible. His major work, *Life-study of the Bible,* comprises over 25,000 pages of commentary on every book of the Bible from the perspective of the believers' enjoyment and experience of God's divine life in Christ through the Holy Spirit. Witness Lee was the chief editor of a new translation of the New Testament into Chinese called the Recovery Version and directed the translation of the same into English. The Recovery Version also appears in a number of other languages. He provided an extensive body of footnotes, outlines, and spiritual cross references. A radio broadcast of his messages can be heard on Christian radio stations in the United States. In 1965 Witness Lee founded Living Stream Ministry, a non-profit corporation, located in Anaheim, California, which officially presents his and Watchman Nee's ministry.

Witness Lee's ministry emphasizes the experience of Christ as life and the practical oneness of the believers as the Body of Christ. Stressing the importance of attending to both these matters, he led the churches under his care to grow in Christian life and function. He was unbending in his conviction that God's goal is not narrow sectarianism but the Body of Christ. In time, believers began to meet simply as the church in their localities in response to this conviction. In recent years a number of new churches have been raised up in Russia and in many eastern European countries.

OTHER BOOKS PUBLISHED BY
Living Stream Ministry

Titles by Witness Lee:

Abraham—Called by God	0-7363-0359-6
The Experience of Life	0-87083-417-7
The Knowledge of Life	0-87083-419-3
The Tree of Life	0-87083-300-6
The Economy of God	0-87083-415-0
The Divine Economy	0-87083-268-9
God's New Testament Economy	0-87083-199-2
The World Situation and God's Move	0-87083-092-9
Christ vs. Religion	0-87083-010-4
The All-inclusive Christ	0-87083-020-1
Gospel Outlines	0-87083-039-2
Character	0-87083-322-7
The Secret of Experiencing Christ	0-87083-227-1
The Life and Way for the Practice of the Church Life	0-87083-785-0
The Basic Revelation in the Holy Scriptures	0-87083-105-4
The Crucial Revelation of Life in the Scriptures	0-87083-372-3
The Spirit with Our Spirit	0-87083-798-2
Christ as the Reality	0-87083-047-3
The Central Line of the Divine Revelation	0-87083-960-8
The Full Knowledge of the Word of God	0-87083-289-1
Watchman Nee—A Seer of the Divine Revelation ...	0-87083-625-0

Titles by Watchman Nee:

How to Study the Bible	0-7363-0407-X
God's Overcomers	0-7363-0433-9
The New Covenant	0-7363-0088-0
The Spiritual Man 3 volumes	0-7363-0269-7
Authority and Submission	0-7363-0185-2
The Overcoming Life	1-57593-817-0
The Glorious Church	0-87083-745-1
The Prayer Ministry of the Church	0-87083-860-1
The Breaking of the Outer Man and the Release ...	1-57593-955-X
The Mystery of Christ	1-57593-954-1
The God of Abraham, Isaac, and Jacob	0-87083-932-2
The Song of Songs	0-87083-872-5
The Gospel of God 2 volumes	1-57593-953-3
The Normal Christian Church Life	0-87083-027-9
The Character of the Lord's Worker	1-57593-322-5
The Normal Christian Faith	0-87083-748-6
Watchman Nee's Testimony	0-87083-051-1

Available at
Christian bookstores, or contact Living Stream Ministry
2431 W. La Palma Ave. • Anaheim, CA 92801
1-800-549-5164 • www.livingstream.com